D0769181

Biotech Investing

Biotech Investing

EVERY INVESTOR'S GUIDE

Jim McCamant

PERSEUS
PUBLISHING

Many of the designations used by manufacturers and sellers to distinguish their products are claimed as trademarks. Where those designations appear in this book and Perseus Publishing was aware of a trademark claim, the designations have been printed in initial capital letters.

Copyright © 2002 by Jim McCamant

All rights reserved. No part of this publication may be reproduced, stored in a retrieval system, or transmitted, in any form or by any means, electronic, mechanical, photocopying, recording, or otherwise, without the prior written permission of the publisher. Printed in the United States of America.

Cataloging-in-Publication Data is available from the Library of Congress
ISBN 0-7382-0509-5

Perseus Publishing is a member of the Perseus Books Group.
Find us on the World Wide Web at http://www.perseuspublishing.com
Perseus Publishing books are available at special discounts for bulk purchases in the U.S. by corporations, institutions, and other organizations. For more information, please contact the Special Markets Department at the Perseus Books Group, 11 Cambridge Center, Cambridge, MA 02142, or call (800) 255-1514 or (617) 252-5298, or e-mail j.mccrary@perseusbooks.com.

Text design by Janice Tapia
Set in 10.75-point Meridien by the Perseus Books Group

First printing, May 2002

1 2 3 4 5 6 7 8 9 10—04 03 02

A few items need clarification before we begin.

This book is intended to help you learn the questions you should ask when making your own decisions about which biotechnology stocks to purchase. With this end in mind, I mention a number of companies in this book, discussing some of them in quite a bit of detail. None of these mentions or discussions should be interpreted, however, as a recommendation to purchase a specific stock. In this fast-moving industry, critical factors (including stock price and the effects of recent industry developments) will inevitably have changed from the time I write. I currently own the stocks of a number of the companies I discuss, but by the time you read this book, I may already have sold them.

Also, everyone who follows the biotechnology industry and keeps track of the number of companies, the amount of financing, or the number of corporate partnerships comes up with different numbers, based on different definitions of which companies are biotech companies. Lacking a single definitive source, I have opted to use what I believe are reasonable, round numbers to emphasize the trends taking place. And for simplicity's sake, I also round some historic stock prices to the nearest dollar or leave them in their original fractions.

Contents

Acknowledgments

First, I want to acknowledge those who came before me in the investment business—their books sparked my interest in investing and helped me learn what makes a successful investor. Benjamin Graham made me realize that the key to investing is determining the value of the company before you buy the stock. Phillip Fisher's *Uncommon Profits Through Common Stocks* helped me realize that growth stocks produce outstanding investment results. Adam Smith's "Money Game" clarified the underlying realities of the investment business in a most entertaining fashion. I also want to thank James L. Fraser, whose newsletter, the *Contrary Investor*, has helped to remind me over the years that it pays to avoid periodic investment fads.

I would not have been able to learn about the biotechnology business without the patience with which many biotech executives have answered my questions over the years. Among the very many, a few stand out above the rest, in part because they helped me learn in the early years: Bob Swanson, Ed Penhoet, George Rathmann, Larry Soll, and Stan Crooke. Also assisting in my continuing education have been the subscribers of the *Medical Technology Stock Letter*, who have asked a lot of good, hard questions over the years. There is nothing like intelligent challenges to help keep thoughts sharp and clear.

For many years, I had thought about writing a book about investing in biotech stocks for the individual investor. However, it was not much more than a thought until I was contacted by an agent, Carol Susan Roth, who had an editor (then at Perseus Publishing) interested in just the book I had been thinking about for years. I thank both of you. I also want to thank the staff at the *Medical Technology Stock Letter:* my son John McCamant, Dick Bailey, and Matt Berry. They not only work hard, they never hesitate to express their own views and keep my thinking from turning sloppy.

The final key ingredient was help in making the book easy and fun to read. For this I am indebted to Alison Marquiss and Ethan Anderson, who have worked diligently and well to reorganize and rewrite this book to make it more accessible.

Biotech
Investing

CHAPTER 1

Why Now Is the Time to Invest in Biotech

Even after twenty years of following biotechnology, my enthusiasm for the industry continues to grow. As I see it, biotechnology offers a marvelous set of characteristics for individual investors. Its companies are making rapid progress in new and exciting areas of science. Its products carry the promise of curing diseases and saving lives, and the demographics driving the demand for them are favorable both in the short and long terms. Its basic market mechanism—physicians requiring treatments for patients—is unaffected by economic cycles. And for the prepared investor, its stocks have the potential to generate outstanding returns.

That said, I've also learned from experience that biotechnology scares off many individual investors. Some are put off by the difficulty of deciphering the science. Others are wary of the built-in uncertainties (and occasional controversies) surrounding one of the key processes of the industry—submitting products for approval by the U.S. Food and Drug Administration (FDA). Still others shy away from the well-known volatility in the prices of biotechnology stocks. So they settle for watching the stocks from the sidelines.

While their concerns are grounded in industry realities, these investors are paying too high a price for their wariness—they're missing out on some of the best long-term returns the markets have to offer. Fortunately, with a little knowledge and the application of a few techniques, individual investors can navigate their way through the difficulties of putting money into this sector and take advantage of these returns.

What's required is viewing the world of biotechnology with a steady investor focus. A working knowledge—not mastery—of the science is all that's needed to invest, and it's well within reach. It's also not necessary to become an industry expert simply to make heads or tails of the FDA approval process or other major operating issues of biotech companies—in many instances, facility with a handful of industry models, case studies, and acronyms is all that's required. As for the volatility of biotechnology stocks, with a modest understanding of the industry and the right investing approach, the individual investor can capitalize on even these slides and surges.

The intent of this book is to take some of the mystery out of the biotechnology sector by surveying its science, history, markets, and investment potential. My hope is that by its end, you might see biotechnology as I do—as a meeting ground between truly inspiring science and versatile capital markets and as one of the great sources of investor value for the next generation.

Theory and Practice: A Performance Example

As an observer of the industry, I believe biotechnology has a promising future, in part because I've already been a beneficiary of its past. I've followed the industry since Genentech's 1980 initial public offering (IPO), and since 1983, I've covered it as cofounder and editor of the *Medical Technology Stock Letter* (MTSL), a newsletter for biotechnology investors.

To illustrate our MTSL recommendations, we created two hypothetical portfolios. We opened the "model" portfolio, a fairly conservative, unleveraged, fully invested "buy and hold" portfolio, in late 1983. We opened the "aggressive" portfolio, a more risky, leveraged portfolio, in mid-December 1987, just two months after the infamous October 19 stock market crash. Since then, we've tracked both portfolios against the Dow Jones Industrial Average.

Before examining the performance of the portfolios versus the Dow, it's worth noting some of the characteristics of the Dow and the biotechnology sector between the end of 1987 and the end of 2001.

Although the Dow has suffered the occasional substantial decline (most notably in October 1989 and during much of 2000–2001), generally speaking, it has continued the rise it began in 1982—the starting date of what is now considered the greatest sustained bull market in the history of the capital markets.

As the Dow continued its upward trend following 1987's Black Monday, the biotechnology sector embarked on a much bumpier ride. Investor enthusiasm and eager capital markets spurred booms in 1987 and 1991, opening doors to a rush of IPOs and rising stars in the sector. Both times, the bubbles burst soon after. The 1991 boom ended in January 1992, a month that also marked the launch of the BTK (an index of biotechnology stocks created by the American Stock Exchange, a surrogate indicator for the entire sector). In an ironic twist, the BTK debuted with a high in January 1992 that it would not approach again until late 1999, despite a strong sustained rally from late 1995 to mid-1996. The 1999 resurgence continued through 2000. In 2001, biotechnology followed the trend of the Dow again, with the BTK dipping 8.5 percent, compared with the Dow's 7.5 percent decline.

To put it simply, across the past fourteen years, the Dow has enjoyed a steady rise, punctuated by a couple of notable corrections. Meanwhile, the biotechnology sector has swung between periods of enthusiasm and fear and endured a slump of nearly eight years along the way.

Yet between December 17, 1987, and the end of 2001, while the Dow rose 421 percent, MTSL's model portfolio grew 940 percent and our aggressive portfolio gained 1,856 percent. During the best bull market run the Dow has ever produced, each of our approaches to biotechnology investing rode out booms and busts to more than double the Dow.

Beyond healthy returns, the successes of the MTSL portfolios contain lessons for the individual investor on future forays into the biotechnology sector. I think the more conservative model portfolio is particularly instructive, because it reflects the kind of long-term, value-investing approach I believe is indispensable to future success in an industry sector where stock prices all too often rise and fall as a result of misunderstandings about what the companies are really doing. On balance, markets will correct for misinformation if given enough time, redeeming and rewarding investors who buy and sell for the right reasons.

Given biotechnology's history and the mechanics of its markets, it seems likely that stock price volatility will remain a feature of the sector going forward. Fortunately, the factors that helped biotechnology weather stock price swings in the past are also still in place. In fact, I believe the fundamentals underlying the industry are as strong as they have ever been, creating an ideal environment for investing.

The Fundamental Appeals of Biotech Stocks

Broadly speaking, biotech stocks are growth stocks. This means their valuations depend on the companies they represent realizing their potential, usually in the form of substantial gains in future earnings. As a growth stock, a thriving biotech is beautiful to behold. A typical successful biotech company not only benefits from an exciting new technology, but it also usually functions as a pharmaceutical company, putting it in a sector with unique advantages. Over the years, pharmaceutical companies have come to be characterized by their consistently high profit margins and high rates of growth. These strengths stem from a series of symbiotic relationships that exist between good science, patent protection, fund-raising ability, market potential, and commitment to research and development, combining to create formidable barriers to entry. The successful biotech operating as a pharmaceutical company enjoys the same advantages and benefits.

The typical flourishing biotech company also shares another characteristic with its pharmaceutical company counterparts: Its markets are evergreen. What's troubling from a human perspective is promising from a market perspective—in short, in any economic climate, people's medical needs remain the same. Economic cycles, one of the main culprits behind stock price movements in other sectors, aren't a factor here.

Biotech's markets aren't just evergreen, they're also growing. People are living longer, and the largest population group in the United States, the baby boomers, is approaching retirement age. As populations age, health care demands tend to increase. Biotech companies are positioning themselves to meet the next waves of demand, gaining ground in their pursuit of treatments for every major cause of illness, including cancer and heart disease. Graying markets are boom markets in biotech.

A good biotech company not only carries the promise of innovative technology, high profit margins, high growth rates, and substantial barriers to entry, but it also on occasion offers its stock at a price the individual investor can afford. From time to time, the biotech sector generates classic bargains—solid companies at low prices, ideal stocks for the fundamental investor.

One of the ironies of biotechnology investing is that the very volatility that prevents many investors from diving into the sector often creates the bargains that disciplined investors seek. Occasionally, when the volatility is sectorwide (rather than company specific), the stocks of some of biotech's finest companies fall into the bargain category—an alarming outcome for the uninformed and a fortuitous one for the prepared.

As in any area of investing, timing is everything. Biotechnology's variation on this theme is that volatility provides multiple chances to get in on a good company. A good example of this is Amgen, one of the industry's flagship companies. Although it would not receive its first product approval until 1989, Amgen went public in 1983, debuting with a market capitalization of $200 million. Across the next few years, as its stock rocketed and dipped, Amgen moved its first product, Epogen (used to treat anemia in patients suffering from kidney failure), through the normal course of clinical trials required for patent approval. MTSL first recommended Amgen in 1985, when the company's market capitalization had tumbled 70 percent from its IPO level. Despite the fact that the company had five products in clinical trials by the end of 1985, the stock continued to be volatile thereafter, providing numerous opportunities for new investors to jump aboard, determined investors to increase their positions, and nervous investors to panic. Over the long run, the value of the company and its products emerged. Today, Epogen is one of Amgen's two powerhouse products, annually generating nearly $2 billion in sales. Less than twenty years after going public, Amgen boasts a market cap that hovers around $70 billion, or roughly 350 times its IPO value.

The speed of Amgen's success highlights an enticing feature of the business of biotechnology: The stars in this sector can rise quickly and grow very bright. At the same time, Amgen is also a good example of another industry truth: The science underlying many of the companies may be cutting-edge, but the business models are often fairly simple.

Formidable as it seems, the market power of Amgen stems in large part from the success of only two drugs (the aforementioned Epogen and Neupogen, used to prevent infections in cancer patients undergoing certain types of chemotherapy). It wasn't until six years after its IPO that Amgen won approval for Epogen; another two years passed before Neupogen was approved. The length of time before the emergence of each product was ample enough for a diligent investor to evaluate Amgen's potential. The periodic volatility affecting the stock during the development stages of each drug afforded the same diligent investor plenty of opportunities to take advantage of Amgen's success. The Amgen example has been repeated many times in biotechnology by companies with one or many products and with market caps both large and small. The science of biotechnology may be advancing rapidly, but the business of the sector moves with a clarity and pace that gives the investor a chance to learn, evaluate, and act.

Biotechnology's Immediate, Promising Future

Most of the basics of the business of biotechnology haven't changed since the industry's beginning nearly thirty years ago. Biotech companies continue to have the potential to generate huge profits using simple business models. They continue to be relatively immune to cyclical effects felt in the rest of the economy. And while the biotech sector as a whole remains subject to the stresses of stock price volatility, the markets over time continue their tendency to recognize intrinsic value in strong companies. A few fundamental changes in the marketplace have had lasting effects on the industry as well, most notably the increase in people's average life spans and the aging of the baby boom generation—twin drivers of current and future upticks in demand for health care products and services.

Beyond these enduring characteristics, I believe there are two even more immediate and compelling reasons why the individual investor should embrace the biotech sector:

1. The science of biotechnology is primed for another explosion. By almost any measure that matters—discoveries, innovations, publications, or patent filings—the pace of advance in existing areas of inquiry is accelerating. In addition, whole new fields of biotechnology are emerging. At present, genomics is the best known of these, but it's only one among several exciting new fields of inquiry that could have transformational effects on the entire industry across the next twenty years.

2. The markets are primed for this explosion. Three decades of experience have given the capital markets the know-how to keep pace with innovation in biotechnology. Right now, as a result of this experience, the cash positions of many biotech companies are extremely strong, and as a whole, the industry has never been better funded. The biotechnology companies of the immediate future will have access to an unprecedented array of options for partnering, merging, acquiring, and assessing "make versus buy" decisions in every step of research, production, and marketing.

The industry is entering a new stage of development. Companies have "grown up" and claimed clear identities, which can be fairly neatly divided into three segments: drugs, diagnostics, and tools. They're exercising more savvy in matching their research and development efforts with market potential. The old trend of biotech companies innovating and then being absorbed by large pharmaceutical companies seems to be giving way to a new model, in which well-managed biotech companies, even small-cap ones, are gaining market power. Now biotech companies are merging and acquiring each other, and they're collaborating with pharmaceutical companies more as a function of marketing efficacy than as a natural result of imbalances in market capitalization.

Finally, the central reason that biotechnology is developing in new and interesting ways—as companies, stocks, and as a sector as a whole—is that this is biotechnology's moment in the sun. Across the next generation, no area of scientific inquiry will have more of an impact on the things we do and the way we live. The age of biotechnology is arriving. With a few tools, there's no reason why the individual investor can't be ready to participate in its profits.

CHAPTER 2

A Map of the Terrain: What Is Biotech?

To most people, biotechnology means developing new drugs. Certainly, drug development is the largest portion of the industry, and it has the potential to reach and help the most people. As a result, it generates the most profits, and thus—from an investor's perspective—holds the most excitement.

But biotech also means industrial and agricultural biotechnology, biotech tools, and biotech diagnostics. Since the beginning of the industry's modern era, marked by the discovery of recombinant DNA in 1973, the term "biotech" has held different meanings for different audiences. From a scientific perspective, the field includes all of the above, extends to the chemical industry, and is even starting to touch materials science, all built on a core of molecular biology with support from the other biological sciences as well as chemistry and physics.

In the investment world, biotech means all young pharmaceutical companies. This includes companies that work solely on drug delivery or drug development without doing the basic drug research themselves. As a practice, biotech investors focus primarily on the drug-related parts of the industry. Investors should, however, understand the characteristics of each category of the biotech sector in order to evaluate their respective opportunities. For while the whole sector benefits from technological advances, each category has its own business model, with different risks and rewards.

Industrial and Agricultural Biotech

Although neither industrial nor agricultural biotech currently offers much opportunity to the individual investor, it's worth examining their limitations before moving on to the meat of the sector. These categories help illustrate the scope of biotech and provide some context for both its past and future.

In their early years, big-name biotech companies such as Genentech, Amgen, and Cetus housed significant industrial biotech programs. They all recognized an opportunity—the potential to replace the industry standard chemical processes of applying heat and pressure with better, cheaper biological methods. Indeed, Genentech's work yielded a joint venture with Corning that (with additional partners and new owners) became the public company Genencor in 2000. Similarly, many industrial enzymes now come from biological processes.

Yet these initiatives did not become industry trends, largely because they didn't offer big profit potential. Most industrial biotech products go for use in outside companies' production processes, and they aren't the only means for making the products. Such customer dependence and interchangeability render these products more cost-sensitive and limit their profits.

The agricultural biotech (agbio) category, already an important factor in crop production, will play an even more significant, positive role in the future of farming. Using genetic modification techniques, agbio improves upon the centuries-old practices of cross-breeding plants and selectively breeding farm animals, isolating and modifying specific genes to produce hardier or faster results in far less time. Agbio also promises to enable farmers to reduce their use of toxic pesticides as they instead use seeds genetically engineered to resist destructive pests.

It will be some time, however, before agbio becomes a good investment area. Negative publicity, stemming from tremendous consumer suspicion and hostility toward genetically engineered plants, has dogged agbio for years. In their efforts to quell this issue, the large chemical companies have made a lot of mistakes, only aggravating it further. Also, most of the smaller, pure agbio companies have been swallowed by large chemical companies, primarily Monsanto and DuPont, making it difficult to evaluate the fraction of the business that actually concerns agbio.

Eventually, agbio will facilitate more efficient production of chemicals and even some drugs. One very exciting possibility—genetically engineering a food to contain a vaccine—would allow cheap, easy vaccinations for the populations of the world's poorer countries.

Tools

Biotech tools include such items as equipment, supplies, or services for drug development; study and analysis software; high-output screening systems; "lab-on-a-chip" technology; DNA arrays; and genomics (the investigation of genes) information. While the biotech and drug companies that purchase these items represent a significant market, it's still relatively small when compared to the large consumer market the drug developers target.

The tools companies' business plans are often likened to the model of selling picks, shovels, and jeans to the miners during the California gold rush rather than digging or panning for nuggets alongside everyone else. You're not going to strike it rich, but you can make a lot of steady money. The problem, in both cases, is competition. The leading tools companies can count on their competitors to match their products within a year. Also, a growing number of drug development biotech companies are trying to build their own tools internally.

When late 1999 and 2000 saw an explosion of initial public offerings for biotech companies, tools companies were well represented. Overall growth in the biotech sector means more new companies, and the new companies need tools to conduct research and develop drugs. Large pharmaceutical companies are also eager customers.

Successful tools companies can make excellent investments, but I have seen excitement over tools companies get out of hand. The most highly valued tools company, Affymetrix, had a 1999 low of $16 per share, a 2000 high of $162 a share (adjusted for splits), and finished out 2000 at $74.44. The pioneer in the DNA chip business, Affymetrix built on technology from the semiconductor business to use chips to help rapidly define gene functions and identify changes in genes, among other services. It's a good technology but a complicated one, with uncertain room for cost reduction and a muddled patent situation as well. Comparing 2000 revenues to total market capitalization ($201 million to more than $8 billion at the peak and $4.3 billion at the end of 2000, both far in excess of the 1:10 ratio that marks the top limit I'll give even superior companies), it's clear that Affymetrix was overvalued. Its 2001 close was $37.75.

Diagnostics

Diagnostics, the technologies used to identify diseases and conditions in patients, constitute the second-largest portion of the biotech industry, right behind drug development. Diagnostics companies can gain profits more quickly than drug developers since they can expect far quicker approval times from regulators, but their profit potential is more limited because of their smaller market.

The biotech industry's first products were diagnostics, as Hybritech and a few other early biotech companies used monoclonal antibodies (immune system proteins that attack invaders, specially produced to all have the same structure and target) to make tests more accurate. With little patent protection, these companies quickly became competitors. Abbott emerged as the leader, and Eli Lilly acquired Hybritech.

Investors periodically get excited about diagnostics companies, but they should be concerned about competition. Since there are few barriers to competition, diagnostics companies are driven to lower product prices to encourage widespread use. Abbott took this route in the mid-1980s, following the discovery that human immunodeficiency virus (HIV) caused acquired immunodeficiency syndrome (AIDS). Several established and new companies worked rapidly to develop tests that would detect the virus in blood and prevent its spread through blood transfusions. Analysts predicted that the blood screening tests would sell between $5 and $10, but competition quickly drove them down to an average of just over $1. No one company had a significant patent position, and Abbott was the best equipped to sacrifice short-term profits to become the dominant market leader. Obviously, such competition makes achieving profitability trickier.

It's rare that a diagnostics company actually has the strong patent position that most claim, but when it does, it stands to profit enormously. Chiron enjoys such a position based on its discovery of the hepatitis C virus in 1986, and the company applies this intellectual property to blood screenings that test directly for HIV and hepatitis C. In just one arm of its screening business (a joint venture with Johnson & Johnson's Ortho Diagnostics division), Chiron collects $80 million in pretax profits each year.

New Drug Development

The biggest and most profitable category of the biotech sector, new drug development is also the most costly. Because it takes years, even decades, to research, test, and produce a product, new drug development requires the most capital to fuel success. But the returns on even a single drug can make a company successful. Drugs typically have gross margins in excess of 80 percent, and several current drugs (including both Amgen's Epogen and Neupogen) have total sales in excess of $1 billion. Add in the minimal competition new drugs face upon their introduction, and companies can see annually increasing revenues, based solely on one drug, until the patent expires.

The crux of biotech investing lies somewhere between those enormous costs and immense returns. To take advantage of the opportunities that are available, investors must first learn to recognize the different types of drugs and understand how their characteristics affect investment value. Most drugs can be classified into one of five general types (explained below): Small molecule drugs, naturally occurring human proteins, monoclonal antibodies, gene therapy, and antisense.

TABLE 2.1 Types of Drugs

Type	Administration	Example
Small molecule drugs	pills	Lipitor
Naturally occurring human proteins	injection	insulin
Monoclonal antibodies	injection	Rituxan
Gene therapy	injection	GVAX
Antisense	injection	Vitravene

Each of these types of drugs represents a different approach to fighting disease, but they can all target the same large disease markets. The two key parameters in a drug's market success—how quickly a drug can be developed and how convenient it will be for patients to use—vary according to the type of drug. Also, some types of drugs present fewer risks during the development process or lend themselves to quick approvals.

Small Molecule Drugs

Historically, large drug companies have focused on the development of small molecule drugs, that is, drugs that can be taken as pills. The small molecule drug market presents several advantages, not least of which is that the drugs are inexpensive to manufacture and thus provide very high profit margins. Small molecule drugs are the work of organic chemists who assiduously design the drugs to have exactly the desired characteristics. These drugs' pill form makes them attractive to patients and doctors alike; patients can use them easily in their own homes and doctors can thus feel confident about patients' compliance. This appeal, along with the fact that the drugs are often prescribed to be taken on a daily basis to treat chronic conditions, means that they have a large target market.

Typically, the first company to bring a small molecule drug to market to treat a particular aspect of disease will secure the largest share of that disease market's revenue and collect substantial profits for the life of its patent. However, the pioneering company can count on its competitors to immediately pursue similar drugs that are not covered by the original patent—using only slightly different chemistry, the competitors go after the same drug target and hope to capture some of the pioneer's market share. Such situations can be the start of patent wars, which we'll look at in a later chapter.

The single largest market for small molecule drugs has been treating various aspects of cardiovascular (heart) disease. Currently, demand is highest for statins, drugs that lower cholesterol levels. In 2001, this class of drugs alone had U.S. sales in excess of $10 billion. A number of older classes of heart drugs, including hypertension drugs, beta-blockers, calcium channel blockers, and ace inhibitors, also continue to have substantial sales. As a group, cardiovascular drugs, most of which are small molecule drugs, have annual U.S. sales of more than $20 billion.

The biggest issue drug companies encountered in their development of small molecule drugs was safety. Unexpected side effects, including toxicity to the liver and kidneys, arose as the companies worked to create drugs that patients could take on a convenient schedule—as often as three times a day, but ideally once a day. To allow daily dosages, the drugs needed to stay in a patient's bloodstream and provide benefit for twenty-four hours before being processed and expelled by the liver and kidneys—without damaging these organs. This meant that the drugs needed longer half-lives (the time it takes for 50 percent of the drug to be cleared from the body). To fulfill this need, specialized drug delivery companies emerged: first Alza, which overcame a rocky beginning to achieve independent success before its acquisition by Johnson & Johnson in 2001 for stock valued at $12 billion; then Elan, an Irish company that built on its drug delivery success to become a full-scale drug company.

Naturally Occurring Human Proteins

The advent of biotechnology made it possible for the first time to make large amounts of naturally occurring human proteins and use them as drugs. Before biotech, the few proteins that were used as drugs came from natural sources. Insulin, the most important, was extracted from animals (mainly pigs), then purified and used to treat type-I diabetics who needed it to survive. Another protein, human growth hormone, was extracted from the pituitary glands of human cadavers, then used to treat children who did not produce enough of it themselves and would have been dwarfs without treatment. Factor VIII, used by hemophiliacs to control their bleeding, was purified from human blood, along with other proteins. Still more proteins were purified from animal sources, including the hormone estrogen, which came primarily from mares' urine.

Still, the manufacture of proteins remains an expensive challenge. The best results come from making most proteins in mammalian cell cultures, which are costly. Others can be made in *e coli* bacteria or yeast, which is less expensive, but may behave differently.

As drugs, proteins currently present one major drawback—they must be injected. If taken by mouth, the digestive system simply treats them as food. Over the last fifteen years, the biotech industry has made major investments in efforts to discover ways to deliver proteins to humans orally, but these have met with only modest success. Other alternate techniques, such as delivering proteins through mucosal membranes of the lungs and mouth, have shown more promise. The first market success for lung delivery will most likely be insulin—Pfizer and Inhale Therapeutics have reached late-stage trials with their test products, and a number of competitors are only a few years behind. Depot delivery of proteins, where a slow, steady release structure allows weekly or monthly rather than daily injections, has shown better results, with Alkermes, Pracesis, and Alza (now part of Johnson & Johnson) leading the field.

While the development of early human protein drugs such as insulin and human growth hormone was straightforward, biotechnology companies encountered more difficulty as they turned to tackle immune system proteins. Some of these drugs, designed to treat cancer, showed promise in animal studies; however, in the substantially more complicated human immune system, tests brought more side effects and higher toxicity rates than researchers expected.

Monoclonal Antibodies

Monoclonal antibodies are also proteins, but they have special properties that make them very useful as drugs. Humans and other mammals naturally produce a wide range of antibodies that attack invasive pathogens as part of their immune responses; monoclonal antibodies are simply large groups of identical antibodies genetically engineered from the same single source. With monoclonal antibodies, scientists essentially direct the cell cultures to produce sizable quantities of the appropriate antibody to attack a specific target.

Monoclonal antibodies rely on some of the same techniques as vaccines, which primarily work by causing the production of human antibodies. Vaccines generate an antibody response, and the immune system retains a memory of this response; then, when attacked by the related pathogen, the body mounts a rapid response, producing both more antibodies and other immune system proteins, with each antibody directed at a specific target.

Like all proteins, monoclonal antibodies currently require injections. Still, they have a large market, because they may play a key role in the treatment of cancer, both alone and in tandem with killing agents such as radioactive isotopes or chemotherapy drugs designed to kill cancer cells, with far fewer side effects. This potential attracted a lot of enthusiasm and media coverage in the late 1980s, but after many false starts and dead ends, commercially viable results have come only recently. The first monoclonal antibody to treat cancer, IDEC Pharmaceutical's Rituxan, gained approval to treat non-Hodgkins (B-cell) lymphoma in late 1997, and its immediate success—$152 million in sales in 1998, its first full year—has illustrated the promise for monoclonal antibodies. Centocor's Remicade, which inhibits the progression of joint damage in patients with rheumatoid arthritis, has also found wide success.

Gene Therapy

Gene therapy also focuses on proteins, but rather than working to deliver the human proteins to the appropriate location in the body (as with naturally occurring human proteins or monoclonal antibodies), gene therapy changes some of the body's genetic code to get it to produce the needed protein itself. In theory, gene therapy can be used to treat any disease that is caused by the insufficiency or lack of a human protein.

Gene therapy holds excellent long-term potential but it faces a number of challenges as it realizes that potential. The biggest challenge is getting the gene into the right target in the body and making it produce the right amount of protein. Initially, scientists did this by creating specific treatments for each individual patient, but this method was expensive and made quality control difficult. Now, most gene therapy work uses genetically modified viruses to deliver the genes to the specific cellular target. Normally, a virus gets into the cell, takes over its machinery, and instructs it to produce more of the virus. With the proper gene added, though, the virus will also cause the cell to produce the desired therapeutic protein. This method has its own drawback—viruses can trigger the body to produce an immune response that may interfere with repeated treatment.

Early enthusiasm over gene therapy focused on its ability to treat diseases caused by genetic defects. Now, more than half of all gene therapy clinical trials target cancer. Not only is this a larger potential market, but it also brings fewer regulatory questions—without treatment, cancer patients face a high likelihood of death, so there is less concern about long-term side effects. I anticipate that the first gene therapy programs to treat cancer will gain approval within the next two to three years.

Antisense

The presence of a protein or too much of a protein can be the culprit in some processes of disease. In these cases, antisense holds the potential to provide an effective drug, because it can stop the production of a protein at the genetic level. This ability can also be used to prevent bacteria or viruses from reproducing. The field has great potential, particularly in treating cancer and inflammatory diseases.

Companies working on antisense ran into difficulty, however, as they tried to achieve a stable antisense molecule and then get that molecule into the cell to do its genetic interference. Chemical changes can affect the stability of the antisense molecule, and potency varies according to delivery method. The industry leader, Isis Pharmaceuticals, has increased stability enough that it recently began human testing of an oral antisense molecule to treat rheumatoid arthritis. To date, however, after ten years of research by several companies in the field, only one drug using antisense technology has gained approval in the United States—Isis's Vitravene, approved to treat cytomegalovirus retinitis in AIDS patients, who can't use traditional therapies to combat the disease, which causes blindness.

Another emerging use for antisense is to help define the function of a newly discovered gene. Once the sequence of a gene is known, scientists can develop an associated antisense molecule that will show what happens when the protein coded by that gene is not produced.

The Lesson

Antisense provides a good illustration of how the investor can look at drug development and recognize that, for each drug type, the risks and rewards will change over time. Although antisense technology has taken longer than expected to commercialize, most of what companies have learned in drug development can be applied to their next drugs. Subsequent drugs, then, will move through the development process more quickly, with significantly higher chances of success. This will likely be the case for the second-generation antisense formulations, which will be delivered as pills.

Similarly, the success of new monoclonal antibody drugs over the past couple of years has significantly reduced the risks associated with developing this type of drug. The key questions now focus not on whether the drug will work, but rather on selecting the right targets and knowing where the competition will be by the time the drug is approved and on the market.

By gaining awareness of the specific traits of different types of drugs, the investor can begin to compare companies, evaluating risks and markets. This will allow the investor to determine how potential reward stacks up against a company's current valuation—and whether its stock is attractive.

CHAPTER 3

An Investor's History of Biotech

In the biotechnology industry, science and finance seem to play off each other. During the start-up phase, biotech companies more closely resemble research labs than product companies, and they can't survive without long time horizons and periodic cash infusions, which the capital markets are eager to provide in exchange for strong (and generally long-term) returns. This interplay between science and financial markets has shaped biotech's history almost since the very beginning. In fact, the biotech industry looks as it does today largely because the investment community drew (and continues to draw) the science of biotechnology out of the laboratory and into the marketplace.

Biotech's Beginnings: Recombinant DNA, Monoclonal Antibodies, and Venture Capitalists

Two scientific breakthroughs launched the modern era of biotechnology. The first became known in 1973, when Herb Boyer of the University of California at San Francisco and Stan Cohen of Stanford published a paper in the *Proceedings of the National Academy of Science*, describing how they successfully extracted DNA from a toad and inserted it into a strain of *e coli*, a common bacterium, which then multiplied and produced the protein encoded by the toad DNA. This feat of genetic engineering was the first successful experiment in recombinant DNA technology, one of the cornerstones of the biotechnology industry. Building on Boyer and Cohen's achievement, scientists used recombinant DNA techniques to quickly grow large amounts of human proteins in yeast, bacterial, and mammalian cells. Biotech's first drugs came out of this rapid generation of naturally occurring human proteins in nonhuman cells. Today, recombinant DNA techniques are what underlie such well-known products as Activase, which is used to treat heart patients; Recombivax, a vaccine for hepatitis B; and Epogen.

Biotechnology's second major breakthrough came from England in 1974, where Cesar Milstein and Georges Kohler discovered how to fuse an antibody-producing cell with a cancer cell, creating a hybridoma that produced large amounts of identical antibodies. Milstein and Kohler's methods paved the way for rapidly growing "monoclonal antibodies" and revolutionized diagnostic testing, which had previously relied on the use of diverse animal antibodies to identify substances in human blood. The innovation of using monoclonal antibodies dramatically increased the accuracy of diagnostic tests while driving down costs, a magical combination in both medical and business terms. Today, monoclonal antibody technology underlies some of biotechnology's biggest-selling products, including home pregnancy tests, one of the first to reach the market.

With the discoveries of Boyer, Cohen, Milstein, and Kohler, modern biotechnology was born. Recognizing the potential of recombinant DNA and monoclonal antibodies, many gifted scientists flocked to the field. The talent infusion spurred further hard work and ingenuity, creating a classic example of a virtuous cycle of scientific innovation that continues to the present day, with each new discovery seemingly leading to the next, transforming the revolutionary into the routine along the way.

The initial excitement of the new field set academia abuzz, and the impact of biotechnology's early breakthroughs soon spread beyond the scientific community. In 1976, Bob Swanson of Kleiner Perkins (one of northern California's first and most successful venture capital firms) phoned Herb Boyer, asking to meet. Boyer's work in recombinant DNA technology intrigued Swanson, and he wanted to propose that he and Boyer start a company. Though Boyer promised Swanson only ten minutes, they talked for three hours, and by the end of their first meeting, they'd agreed to start Genentech, the first biotech company.[1]

In retrospect, it seems almost natural that the transition of biotechnology from a science into an industry took place in northern California. The region features an indispensable combination of leading universities to provide the scientific talent and a vibrant venture capital industry that, during the 1970s, had already started to prosper by financing electronics companies. The early successes in electronics bolstered the resolve of venture capitalists in the new science of biotech, allowing them to provide relatively easy access to capital and impart an entrepreneurial tradition to what had essentially been (at least in its first two years) a pure laboratory science.

As the first of its kind, Genentech faced all of the challenges of a trailblazer. The need for a long time horizon and the cash to fund it were self-evident, but how to go about securing each was less obvious. Using recombinant DNA technology, the company developed its first two offerings in rapid succession: a human insulin product in 1978 and a human growth hormone (HGH) product in 1979. While these advances were encouraging, revenues were a long way off; both products faced the long waiting period for FDA approval before they could be introduced to the public. Nonetheless, powered by the promise of its early laboratory successes (as well as a partnership with Eli Lilly for the development of human insulin), Genentech began the era of biotech as a public investment vehicle when it announced its initial public offering (IPO) in the fall of 1980. Paine Webber and Hambrecht & Quist underwrote the offering and watched as investors jumped on the stock during the opening day of trading. Genentech, which priced its offering at $35 per share, saw the stock leap as high as $80 in early trading before closing at $70 at the end of its first day. The dot-com phenomenon has since inured investors to this kind of opening-day activity, but in 1980 Genentech's performance was remarkable, setting a record for the largest first-day advance for an IPO. It was an unprecedented debut, one that sent the capital markets a memorable message: Investors were ready to buy into biotechnology companies, even ones that were years away from generating earnings.

In addition to providing Genentech with badly needed funding for its promising products, the success of its IPO galvanized venture capitalists, investment banks, and biotech scientists alike. Out of their numbers, a new breed emerged—biotech entrepreneurs. The first and perhaps most notable group of these were the venture capitalists, led by Bill Bowes, who took the initiative to start Amgen. Bowes built the company as if it were an ambitious start-up in almost any other industry: He located the scientists he wanted in southern California, recruited them, and then set about the task of convincing George Rathmann to run the company. With the pieces in place, Bowes and Rathmann looked for venture financing, a task Genentech's early success had made much easier. Amgen raised $19 million in its initial round of venture funding in January 1981, a very large sum for an early round. Rathmann insisted that if they were going to develop the business properly, they should not have to worry about money for at least a couple of years.

Part of what drove Rathmann's urgency was the sudden jump in entrepreneurial activity in biotechnology. The science seemed to be turning into an industry almost overnight, and Rathmann wanted to partner with or acquire some enticing new biotech properties. During Amgen's formation, Bowes and Rathmann considered working with a group of scientists and entrepreneurs who had begun an instrument business that became Applied Biosystems. They also had serious discussions with a small group of scientists from the University of California at San Francisco who had worked toward developing the first hepatitis B vaccine using recombinant DNA technology, but an agreement never materialized, and the UCSF scientists began their own company, Chiron, incorporating in May 1981. The same month, Cetus, an early biotech company focused on industrial applications, went public and raised an impressive $120 million. Important companies were springing into existence, and private and public markets were responding. Biotech was experiencing its first boom.

The First Product Wars

Throughout the boom of 1980 and 1981, modern biotech's first company remained ahead of the curve. Genentech boasted the first scientific breakthrough (recombinant DNA technology) and the first IPO success. And it was the first biotech company to head into the uncharted waters of launching and marketing products.

Genentech's initial strategy was fluid: It would develop and market products on its own whenever possible but collaborate with large drug companies when it needed more marketing firepower than it could muster with its own resources. For the development of its first product, Genentech opted for the collaborative route, seeking out Eli Lilly to handle the marketing.

Using recombinant DNA techniques, Genentech scientists had cloned human insulin in 1978. The company then licensed the technology to Eli Lilly in exchange for research support and future royalties. The arrangement allowed Genentech to focus its resources on research, shifting the burden of marketing its first product to Eli Lilly's experienced marketing division. When it gained approval from the Food and Drug Administration in 1982, Genentech's human insulin product (Humulin) scored a double coup: As the first human protein produced using recombinant DNA technology, it served as powerful proof of biotechnology's ability to produce marketable drugs; and from the revenues it generated from the licensing agreement with Lilly, it gave Genentech a product-based income stream, allowing the company to expand its research on other potential products. The first collaboration between unequal partners— an emerging biotech and a giant pharmaceutical company—had made winners of both.

Genentech continued its rapid progress in 1979, using recombinant DNA technology to produce human growth hormone (HGH). This proved to be a great product for a biotech company. First, HGH had an unusual application: It was (and still is) used to help children who don't produce enough growth hormone naturally, a rare condition that, if untreated, can lead to dwarfism. The HGH market was also the definition of a niche market, as the product held extremely high value for a modest number of patients and prescribing physicians. Better still, Genentech's version of HGH had near-perfect market timing. Prior to Genentech's innovation, the source for HGH had been the pituitary glands of cadavers, but as Genentech developed its product, scientists discovered that cadaver-extracted HGH carried the risk of transmitting Creutzfeldt-Jakob disease (the human version of bovine spongiform encephalopathy, or mad cow disease), and it was withdrawn from the market. By the time Genentech's version of HGH (Protropin) earned FDA approval, its only competition in the market had disappeared.

The combination of these factors led Genentech to take a different course with HGH than the one it had chosen for the launch of its human insulin product. In 1985, Genentech brought its HGH product to market as the first recombinant pharmaceutical to be manufactured and marketed by a biotechnology company. It was an ideal product to test the concept that a biotech could produce and sell its own products. HGH served a relatively narrow market (mostly pediatric endocrinologists) that could be managed by a small sales force. When the product was launched, it had no rival in the marketplace; Eli Lilly was developing its own version but Genentech had a significant head start. The looming competition over the HGH market would settle the question of what mattered most—first mover advantage or deep marketing pockets.

When Eli Lilly's HGH product gained FDA approval a year and a half after Genentech's, most analysts predicted that Lilly would soon dominate the market. Not only was Lilly a far larger company with vastly superior sales experience, but its product was also marginally superior to Genentech's. Lilly's product was an exact duplicate of the natural human protein, whereas Genentech's version had one extra amino acid at the end.

Despite its advantages and the analysts' predictions, Lilly couldn't overcome Genentech's head start. The young biotech company maintained its dominant position, and Lilly never captured more than a third of the market. Genentech's success proved to the capital markets that, at least in niche plays, biotech companies could do a good job of marketing their own drugs and defending their share against big pharmaceutical companies.

Against the backdrop of Genentech's early market successes, biotech moved into its second boom in 1983. California Biotechnology (now known as Scios), Immunex, and Biogen all came public during this period. But this was a short-lived market enthusiasm, powered in part by the emergence of promising new biotech companies as well as the sudden success of IPOs in the electronics industry—for a time, it seemed, any stock having to do with anything technological looked attractive to investors. Amgen had its IPO in June 1983, toward the end of the boom, but it still opened at $18 per share, a substantial jump from the $4 per share paid by Rathmann and Bowes's group of venture capitalists in January 1981. This price was all the more impressive given that the company still had no product. The $42 million the IPO generated allowed Rathmann to realize his goal of aggressively pursuing product development without short-term financial pressure.

By August 1983, the markets had begun to cool off. Chiron, the company founded by UCSF scientists, had hoped to raise $30 million with its IPO, but in the end only garnered $18 million, signaling the start of a postboom hangover. Many stocks declined to levels well below their initial offering prices. In late 1984, Chiron slid to $4.50, down from an IPO listing of $12, and Amgen fell to less than $4 per share. The slump gave public investors the chance to buy Amgen's stock at the same $4 price venture capitalists had paid in early 1981. After the lows in late 1984, the stocks gradually worked their way higher, but without much excitement.

With the surges and slides of the early 1980s, biotech learned its first lessons in the capital markets. Investors gained experience with the changeable nature of biotech stocks, and biotech entrepreneurs learned the importance of raising money when the market is eager to dole it out. Or, as Amgen's George Rathmann once put it, "If you want hors d'oeuvres, you better take them when they're passing them out." Savvy analysts took note as well, identifying the first evidence of what would become a characteristic discrepancy in the biotech industry: While the science steadily advanced, the stock prices didn't always follow suit.

The Next Wave

The next sustained surge in biotech stocks peaked in mid-1987, powered in part by the excitement surrounding monoclonal antibodies. A dozen years had passed since Milstein and Kohler's breakthrough research in England, and during that time, research had advanced to the point where monoclonal antibodies seemed poised to become the next great weapon in the fight against cancer. An antibody could be designed to home in on a specific target—a protein unique to cancer cells known as an antigen. The implications caught the attention of the medical community, the biotech sector, the capital markets, and the media: By attaching some sort of killing agent to them, antibodies could be transformed into "magic bullets," capable of seeking out and destroying cancer cells with only minimal side effects for the patients.

The prospect of a cure for cancer had rippled through the industry. In late 1985, Eli Lilly had agreed to acquire Hybritech, a San Diego–area company founded in 1978 with initial financing from Kleiner Perkins. Even though Hybritech's strength in monoclonal antibodies lay more in the area of developing new diagnostic tests, the potential for cancer treatments helped drive the $300 million deal. Bristol Myers, the leading supplier of drugs for cancer treatment, was worried enough about the Lilly deal to make a comparable offer to Genetic Systems, a Seattle-area monoclonal antibody company.

The two $300 million deals created a swarm of rumors about other possible acquisitions of biotech companies by large drug companies. In addition, the Hybritech-Lilly deal triggered a burst of biotech start-ups in San Diego, most of which involved key people from Hybritech. Following the two deals, many analysts and industry insiders predicted a general trend—aggressive acquisitions would lead to the assimilation of the new biotech industry into the older, more established market structure of the big pharmaceuticals.

Genentech also did its part to help fuel the biotech boom of 1987, with the successful clinical development of Activase (TPA), which was approved by the FDA and introduced late in the year. Activase helped to limit the damage from heart attacks by dissolving blood clots, and Genentech management was high on the product from the beginning, encouraging analysts to project more than $500 million in annual sales within a few years. After its early success with marketing HGH into a small niche, Genentech seemed ready to make history again, launching Activase as the first potential blockbuster drug developed and marketed by a biotech company.

Activase was following on the heels of another promising Genentech product, alpha interferon, which received approval in 1986. Interferons were natural human proteins that acted to stimulate an immune response; the initial target for Genentech's interferon product, in keeping with the times, was cancer. Genentech licensed

TABLE 3.1

Companies founded by former Hybritech employees have fueled the growth of the San Diego biotech industry. The following four companies had initial public offerings in 1991, and many more have followed.

Company	Amount Raised	Market Capitalization	
		After IPO	Recent
IDEC Pharmaceuticals	$45 million	$121 million	$8.3 billion
Genta	$25 million	$117 million	$725 million
Isis Pharmaceuticals	$25 million	$104 million	$785 million
Cytel	$52 million	$166 million	NA

Note that all but Isis were founded by former Hybritech executives, and by 1991 the total market cap of the remaining three exceeded the $300 million Lilly paid for Hybritech.

its alpha interferon to Hoffmann–La Roche in 1986, a move matched by Biogen, which produced a competing interferon product (also targeting cancer) and then licensed it to Schering-Plough. In the midst of its next wave, biotech's leading company was rolling out products to treat heart and cancer patients, addressing broad social needs and huge medical markets at the same time.

Biotech and big pharmaceutical companies alike followed Genentech's lead and often crossed paths in interesting ways. In 1987, Merck received approval to market a vaccine for hepatitis B, the first vaccine to use recombinant DNA technology. The vaccine had followed a circuitous route from conception through to the FDA, based on work that had begun at the University of California at San Francisco and concluded at Chiron (Merck paid royalties to both). In 1988, Amgen had its first landmark product approval for Epogen, the product name for EPO. Amgen retained the right to sell Epogen to kidney dialysis patients suffering from anemia, but licensed the rights for other indications in the United States, as well as foreign rights outside of Asia, to Johnson & Johnson.

During 1986 and 1987, the combination of sharp advances in the prices of biotech stocks and increased media attention again created another good period for biotech IPOs, as well as secondary offerings for companies that had already gone public and were beginning to run short of cash. Among the companies that came public in 1986–1987 were a number of the other private biotech companies that specialized in monoclonal antibodies, including Xoma and ImClone Systems. It was also a favorable time for biotech start-ups, as venture capitalists were willing to make new biotech investments after having taken profits on earlier investments within the sector.

As all booms do, biotech's third boom ended, drawing to a close in late 1987. Many biotech stocks fell during the October 1987 crash; in fact, during the fourth quarter of 1987, Genentech's stock was the only biotech that didn't drop at least 50 percent from its summertime high. Amgen tumbled from $46 to $16 and Chiron slipped from $37 to $8. Then, in 1988, Activase's failure to meet analyst estimates finally pulled Genentech down with the rest. Biotech's pioneering company saw its stock fall to $14. There was an ironic element in Genentech's decline: Activase was a successful product from the outset, but Genentech's own management had overhyped its prospects to the analysts, setting the company up for a fall. Though Activase sales would eventually peak at $300 million annually, the product missed analyst targets from the very beginning. And Genentech couldn't make up for the shortfall with its alpha interferon product, because Schering-Plough had wisely shifted the focus for its own interferon product from cancer (where it ultimately proved only modestly effective) to hepatitis C. The net result: Schering dominated the hepatitis market, and Genentech found itself suffering from its first truly costly market misstep.

The mistakes with Activase and interferon cost Genentech its position as the market leader in biotechnology, a position it relinquished to Amgen in 1988 and never regained. Epogen, Amgen's first product offering, carried Rathmann's company to its current dominant position. Epogen is now the largest selling biotech product in the world, with Amgen's and Johnson & Johnson's combined 2000 sales totaling $4.7 billion. By the end of 1988, venture capitalists and investors no longer talked of finding the next Genentech. They spoke instead of finding the next Amgen.

The final fallout of the end of the 1987 boom came in the merger arena. In light of the stock market crash and the failure of interferon to treat cancer, the Hybritech and Genetic Systems deals ended up as major disappointments for the buyers (Lilly and Bristol Myers, respectively). The failures of these deals discouraged big pharmaceuticals from acquiring biotech companies outright. Although a few partial acquisitions took place (most notably between American Cyanamid and Immunex, and American Home Products and Genetics Institute), the predicted wave of biotech acquisitions by large drug companies never really materialized. To date, most acquisitions within the sector feature biotech companies buying other biotech companies.

The 1990s: A Boom, a Long Slump, and the Sector Takes Shape

By 1991, the biotech sector seemed to be operating in regular four-year investment cycles. A surge in stock prices in 1991 mimicked similar moves in 1987 and 1983. Tops are easier to identify than bottoms, and with one top in June 1983 and the next in the second quarter of 1987, a pattern seemed to be developing. However, with a good year under way in 1991, the group continued to work its way higher. This resulted in an excellent year for the biotech stocks, particularly among companies with products in late-stage clinical trials.

Investors were still looking for the next Amgen. Amgen's stock was up more than three and a half times for the year, thanks largely to the successful introduction of its second drug, G-CSF. Sold as Neupogen, G-CSF treated cancer patients whose white blood cells had been depleted as a side effect of chemotherapy. By boosting their white cell counts, Neupogen allowed cancer patients to continue to receive their chemotherapy and helped protect them from infections. Neupogen and Epogen proved that a biotech company could produce more than one huge success, and the combination of these two products cemented Amgen's position as biotech's new front-runner. Neupogen's success was also testimony to the excellence of Amgen's marketing arm; Amgen's product consistently outsold a rival product (GM-CSF, developed by Immunex) that by some indications was a superior offering to Neupogen. Amgen had become biotech's first truly dominant company—it didn't need a first-mover advantage, only a fairly competitive product to win in the marketplace.

The 1991 boom featured other product advances, most notably Baxter winning approval for a recombinant version of a blood factor used to treat patients suffering from hemophilia type A. But the real story of the year, besides Amgen, was the crop of IPOs it produced. The start-ups born during the venture-funding frenzy of 1987 went public in 1991 and early 1992. A total of thirty-eight biotech offerings raised a combined $1.2 billion, and the capital markets poured another $2.5 billion into secondary offerings. To put this in perspective, compare it to April 1989, when the top twenty-five biotech companies had a total market capitalization of only $4.6 billion.[2]

The top of this cycle came around the end of January 1992, four and a half years after the previous peak. Both the American Stock Exchange and the Chicago Board Option Exchange created biotech indexes on which investors could trade options. The indexes made it easier to track the price action of biotech stocks as a group, but the excitement that led to their creation also marked a top for biotech stocks. While the American Stock Exchange Index (symbol BTK) remains one of the more effective ways to follow what is going on in the biotech sector, the CBOE index quietly disappeared a couple of years ago without any public announcement. An investor with only a casual interest in the group would have done well if he had sold the biotech group when this index was created and then repurchased when it ended.

The decline from the 1992 peak was one of the largest and longest in the history of the biotech industry. Despite a good rally in late 1995 to mid-1996, the BTK index did not pass its January 1992 high until 1999. In addition to the hangover that always comes when investors get too excited about any sector, a number of the companies that had attracted the most attention saw their products fail in late-stage clinical trials. Two of these, Xoma and Centocor (since acquired by Johnson & Johnson), had unsuccessfully attempted to use similar monoclonal antibodies to treat sepsis. When Synergen tried a somewhat different approach to treat sepsis and fell short as well, biotech investors were no longer in a mood to anticipate good news from clinical trials.

In 1994, talk about changing the U.S. health care system, led by Hillary Clinton, created uncertainty about the possibility of price controls on drugs and accelerated the decline. The ensuing speculation led to the clearest bottom in the history of biotech stocks to date, in the autumn of 1994.

Near the bottom, a number of interesting things happened to the sector. First, at the end of June 1994, one of the largest biotech-focused hedge funds announced that it would close and return funds to investors. Then, the Oppenheimer Global Biotech Fund, the best-performing mutual fund of 1991, changed its name to the Oppenheimer Global Developing Growth Fund. In both cases, this resulted in the liquidation of biotech holdings, which exerted further downward pressure on biotech stock prices. Finally, in September, *BusinessWeek* ran a cover story with the headline "Biotech: Why It Hasn't Paid Off."

The lead article stated, in its second paragraph, "After a giddy run in the early '90s, 'the market is disillusioned' with biotech, declares Karen Firestone, who manages Fidelity Investments' $500 million Select Biotechnology Fund. From Wall Street's perspective, 'the technology hasn't worked, and the likelihood of success is lower.'"

Two paragraphs further down, the journalist really heaped it on: "Instead, the industry has been hamstrung by uneven management, driven by greed to lure new investment and form companies that have little prospect of succeeding, and wracked by product failures. Even if the market warms up again, consolidation is inevitable.

"'Seventy percent of these companies need to go out of business,' argues Lisa B. Tuckerman, who from her Montana base analyzes biotech for the New York investment management fund at Spears, Benzak, Salomon & Farrell. More and more executives in an industry renowned for its optimism agree.

"The best of the technology will survive, but primarily inside large drugmakers, not in an independent industry. 'Nobody's going to make it alone,' contends Genentech chief executive G. Kirk Raab, who came to that realization in 1990, when he sold 60% of his company to Roche Holdings Ltd."

Only the diligent reader who got to the end of the article, which discussed some biotech successes, would see that there was any hope for the industry. Indeed, the grim news of biotech's demise turned out to be premature. Beneath the gloomy predictions of 1994, the science of biotechnology continued apace. The introduction of new products continued to accelerate, with a gradual shift away from naturally occurring human proteins to other types of products. One example of this trend was the approval in 1997 of Agouron's Viracept, a protease inhibitor to treat HIV. It was not the first drug of this class to be approved, but it rapidly became the market leader, and Agouron reaped the benefit when it was acquired by Warner Lambert (now part of Pfizer) in 1999 for $2.1 billion. Another key 1997 approval was that of Rituxan, a drug developed by IDEC Pharmaceuticals to treat B-cell lymphoma. After all the misfires of the 1980s, Rituxan was the first monoclonal antibody to be approved to treat cancer.

Underneath the cover of the 1992–1999 slump, biotech began to assume its current shape as an industry. The sector grew to boast over 300 publicly traded companies, pushing a steadily increasing number of products through late-stage clinical trials. (The number of new biotech drugs approved each year now exceeds the total developed annually by the traditional pharmaceutical industry.) As the scientific innovation continued, the fundamentals of the companies improved, setting the stage for a recovery, which finally gathered momentum in 1999.

The March 2000 Top and the Financing Boom

Riding on the coattails of an overheated high-tech stock market, biotech stocks broke out of their prolonged slump in 1999, peaking in early March 2000. This top was unique for how fast the stocks moved up as they neared the peak and how quickly most retreated after reaching it. The sector was led both up and down by the genomics stocks and the media publicity about the sequencing of the human genome. Then, when investors were looking for a reason to sell, President Clinton and Prime Minister Blair made their joint statement, saying that "To realize the full promise of the research, raw fundamental data on the human genome, including the human DNA sequence and its variations, should be made available to scientists everywhere." There was nothing new or negative in the statement, but investors interpreted it as raising doubts about the viability of patents in the biotech sector, despite accompanying positive assertions about intellectual property's "important role in stimulating the development" of

TABLE 3.2 Biotechnology Index (BTK), 2000–2001
Month-to-Month vs. Annualized Return

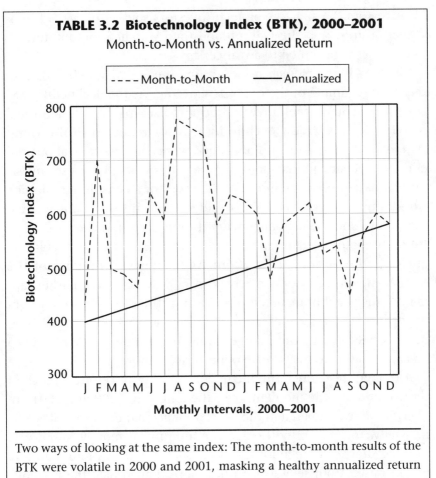

Two ways of looking at the same index: The month-to-month results of the BTK were volatile in 2000 and 2001, masking a healthy annualized return of 21.1 percent across the two-year period.

new products. The statement triggered a sharp sell-off. Despite this drop, the biotech sector ended up with an excellent price performance for the year: The BTK rose 62 percent for the year and the NASDAQ biotech index (symbol NBI) rose 23 percent.[3]

Looking at the market action of biotech stocks in 2000, one of the most striking features is the amount of volatility exhibited by individual stocks. Many interesting mid- and small-cap biotech companies moved up as much as ten times from their 1999 lows, then experienced declines of more than 80 percent from their highs. This generated a lot of excitement but it also made it difficult for investors. Most active biotech investors sold all or part of individual positions on the way up and then watched, dumbfounded, as the stocks continued to advance.

The lows in the biotech stocks around the end of March 2001 presented an example of the opposite extreme. As the decline in NASDAQ passed 50 percent, investors began to get frightened—a normal reaction to the largest decline in a major index since the Great Depression. Falling technology stock prices and worries about the effect of the slowing economy on earnings created a tense investment environment, where many investors considered biotech stocks' historic volatility and decided they did not want to own them any longer. This happened without any significant bad news from the biotech sector, and it was clearly a result of fear replacing greed as the dominant emotion. At the lows, a number of the smaller cap biotech stocks reached prices at which their market capitalizations roughly matched their cash in the bank. These types of opportunities have appeared periodically, at each low in the past, but it is possible that the changes in the investment world may keep volatility high and thus create opportunities more often.

Although the short-term fluctuations in stock prices drew much of the attention in the moment, over the long run, 2000 and 2001 are likely to be remembered as the years in which biotech came of age financially. In 2000 in particular, the amount of money raised was nothing short of tremendous. In fact, 2000's total of more than $37 billion raised from selling securities more than tripled the previous year's figure (interestingly, a large chunk of 1999's $11 billion total came in the fourth quarter, which many industry players would include as part of the same biotech financing cycle). In February 2000 alone, biotech raised $6 billion in new capital, a sum that exceeded the annual total of any year in biotech's history up until 1999. So formidable was 2000's performance that 2001 has been maligned as a poor financing year in comparison, even though it will rank as biotech's second most productive fund-raising year in the industry's brief history, with a projected annual total of $12 billion flowing into the coffers of new and established companies.

The inflows of cash from 2000 and 2001 have set the stage for biotech's next era. Because of the financing boom, biotech companies not only have seen their risk of running out of capital dramatically reduced, they've also been given a significant boost in flexibility in executing their business plans. For one thing, the number of partnerships between small and large biotech companies is likely to increase. And the larger biotech companies, emboldened by strong cash positions, will have more choice in whether or not to partner in "make" decisions (developing drugs in-house) and will be more aggressive in "buy" situations (acquiring technologies or companies whose services fit their needs). Thus, while biotech and its many exciting technologies—genomics and stem cell technology, to name two—have captured the attention of investors and the media, I believe that the single most important development for biotech in 2000 was the record amount of capital that flowed into the industry.

A Last Look Back

What can the individual investor take away from nearly thirty years of biotech history? Quite a few points. The sector's consciousness is informed by the stories of Genentech and Amgen, the breakthroughs in recombinant DNA, monoclonal antibodies, and now, perhaps, genomics. Biotech companies have learned their marketing lessons from the war stories of their predecessors. Among these lessons: Fledgling biotech companies can market niche products internally, and they can collaborate with large pharmaceuticals to reach bigger markets. And despite twenty years of speculation and market mood swings, biotech companies do not appear to be on the verge of being swallowed up en masse by large pharmaceutical companies. Small biotech companies can become big biotech companies on the strength of one blockbuster product; Amgen, the current industry leader, stakes its claim to dominance on the strength of just two blockbuster products.

Individual investors can also follow the lead of venture capitalists, who now have enough experience with the periodic jumps and slumps in the biotech sector to know when to increase their positions and when to stay the course. And true students of biotech recognize that the gaps between stock price and scientific advances, while trying, are not everlasting. The market eventually recognizes value and punishes miscues, even in a sector with as much volatility as biotech—a revelation we'll examine in further detail in the next chapter.

Notes

1. Cetus was formed by Ron Cape and Peter Farley in Berkeley in 1971 (predating Genentech), but the company's primary focus was in industrial applications, and thus it is not generally regarded as the progenitor of the modern biotech industry.
2. It is interesting to look at the price action of this group of stocks now that they have almost ten years of price performance. Remembering the excitement and the sharp declines that most of the stocks made in 1993–1994, I was surprised that the average performance for this group of thirty-eight stocks has been excellent in total, although most of them dropped well below their IPO price in 1994–1995. IDEC Pharmaceuticals, ImClone Systems, ICOS, MedImmune, and Sepracor have posted big gains, more than making up for the shortfalls of the few losers within the group.
3. The main difference between the two indexes: The NBI covers all the larger biotech stocks traded on NASDAQ and is weighted by market capitalization, which means it is dominated by the larger capitalization companies. Amgen, for example, represents more than 30 percent of the index.

CHAPTER 4

Investing Philosophy: How It Works and Why It Matters in Biotech

When thinking about any kind of personal investing, it's tempting to focus entirely on mechanics. There's a straightforward, step-by-step appeal to starting with a basic understanding of what a sector does and how it works, then moving on to deeper research into individual companies, and finishing with the identification of worthwhile stocks. Although this approach can work in other sectors, I don't believe it's enough in biotechnology. The mechanics may be essential to making good biotech investment decisions, but so is another less tangible element: an investing philosophy—in other words, a small, versatile set of rules to guide buy, sell, and hold decisions.

In any sector, viewing any facet of investing through the lens of a sound philosophy enables the individual investor to see the forest for the trees. It sharpens each step of the mechanics, from conceptualization to company research to stock selection. And in biotechnology, it can also mean the difference between success and failure. As such, it's worth taking a brief detour from the mechanics to examine what makes an effective investing philosophy and look at how much it really matters when it's applied in the markets.

General Principles:
The Foundation of My Investing Philosophy

I believe in long-term value investing.

I think markets operate rationally in the long run, even though they often feed on emotion in the short run.

I think the difference between company risk and stock price risk is critical to making investment decisions.

I think the most attractive balance between investment risk and reward is found when what I've learned about a company goes against the conventional wisdom of the markets.

These beliefs combine to make me what I am: an avid follower of growth stocks, a frequently contrarian investor, and a biotechnology enthusiast. They're time- and market-tested, having grown out of ideas and strategies I've come across and put to use during my forty years in the investment business. And they've become the foundation for the set of rules that make up my own investing philosophy.

I have six rules that I use as touchstones for any investing decision. Taken as a group, they make up an investing philosophy that's particularly well suited for investing in biotechnology. Properly applied, they help cut through the many traps that the biotechnology sector lays for the individual investor. I'll go through the rules one at a time later in this chapter, but before examining them, it helps to take a closer look at the conditions in biotechnology that make them so valuable.

Biotech Confusion

As a sector, biotechnology suffers from two interrelated (and apparently inexhaustible) sources of confusion. The first stems from too little information—the vast majority of its companies aren't profitable, a shortcoming that obscures their true value. The second stems from too much information—the industry sometimes feels as if it's overrun with conflicted experts doling out conflicting analyses. The interplay of these twin sources of confusion can have a significant impact on market valuations and waylay the unprepared investor.

A single statistic crystallizes the problem behind the first source of confusion: Among the 300 or so publicly traded biotech companies, currently only about 10 percent are profitable. The number of profitable companies continues to increase rapidly, but the current percentage is low relative to other sectors.

Obviously, the less a company can be measured and evaluated using traditional financial metrics, the more subjective investor evaluations of that company will be. The perceived difficulty of valuing unprofitable companies causes many investors to either avoid the sector entirely or invest with a high level of anxiety. Both approaches are unfortunate, especially in biotechnology, where the biggest determinants of success among as-yet-unprofitable companies lie within the products they're developing. There are methods to assess the chances of products succeeding and to estimate the size of the markets they might serve that can be effective substitutes for traditional financial measures (we'll examine these further in chapters to follow).

Wary investors are often conservative and either don't know about these proxies or take little comfort in them. They're also unmoved by the notion that, in biotechnology, lack of profitability doesn't mean the same thing as it does in other industries. And they are not often swayed by the argument that biotech companies operate within a proven business model that often calls for public and private financing far in advance of product approvals and patent-protected profits.

As a result of these views, when these investors do chose to put money into biotechnology, they tend to react more drastically to the latest market developments, helping to create a self-fulfilling prophecy. In conventional terms, unprofitable biotech companies seem more risky. Investors holding this view tend to overreact to news in the markets because of the perceived risk, which affects stock prices, which in turn makes the companies appear even more risky.

Biotech's second source of confusion is its experts—scientists, investment analysts, and journalists working within the industry. Most of them are good at what they do, and if accessed properly, the information they provide can be quite useful. Then again, because their roles within the sector are frequently misunderstood, biotechnology insiders often hurt the decisionmaking process of the individual investor.

Scientists (usually industry insiders) often intimidate investors. But it's been my experience that their takes on the industry are frequently misleading. When they comment on the quality of the science within their own companies and among competitors, they're perceived as experts by many investors, and their opinions can have dramatic short-run effects on stock prices. Intuitively, this process makes sense—one would think that biotechnologists would be extremely well qualified to evaluate biotechnology companies. However, there's a catch: The field of biotechnology is now so broad that any given scientist can become an expert only in the details of a small part of the field. In other words, the scope of a biotechnology expert is narrow and there are few investment decisions in biotech where it is necessary to make fine scientific decisions.

As a result, the individual investor's problem with scientists boils down to a case of mistaken identity: The markets perceive scientists as broad experts on biotechnology, when in fact they're specialists, often with areas of expertise too narrow to fairly assess the breadth of the science in the companies they're analyzing. In the short run, whether they're right or wrong, their pronouncements are taken seriously and often increase the volatility of stock prices within the sector.

When it comes to Wall Street analysts, the problem for the individual investor is one of mixed motives. Both buy-side and sell-side analysts can significantly influence short-term stock prices—a power that in itself isn't troubling, except for the fact that what drives the typical Wall Street analyst is almost never in line with what motivates the individual investor.

While the individual investor simply seeks to maximize return relative to risk, the Wall Street analyst has more complicated objectives. The sell-side analyst who works for an investment bank or a brokerage house is paid large bonuses for attracting investment banking business to his or her firm. At times this can conflict with the sell-side analyst's main job of recommending stocks on their investment potential alone. Under these circumstances, investors who put their full faith in the advice of sell-side analysts risk being undermined by ulterior motives.

In addition, sell-side analysts often have a hard time recommending the selling of one of their winners, even one that's exceeded its target price. So they sustain their buy ratings by focusing their reports on the positives, and since in any given company there's always something that's going well, this isn't a difficult task. Of course, the reverse happens when a stock a sell-sider has been recommending goes down. Then the analyst focuses on reasons for the decline, and since every company has flaws, this too is an easy task.

The unfortunate net effect of the sell-sider's approach is obvious: When stocks are already near their lows, they're downgraded, and when they're nearing their highs, they're recommended—exactly the wrong advice for an individual investor, especially one betting on the short term. As a result, the individual investor gets in or stays out at precisely the wrong time, thereby contributing to the volatility of the markets.

Meanwhile, the buy-side analyst (who usually works for a mutual fund or a hedge fund) is under constant pressure to beat the Street—to outperform competing buy-side analysts, mutual fund managers, and the S&P 500—often over very short time periods. In a good situation, under great pressure to produce, a buy-side analyst may take many short-term investing risks an individual investor would never consider. Buy-side analysts can get carried away with greed as prices rise and gripped with fear as prices decline. Locked in an endless short-term competition with their peers, buy-siders can elevate the peaks and deepen the troughs of frenzied markets by overbidding or dumping stocks, thereby testing the resolve of the individual investor.

Like Wall Street analysts, journalists also have objectives that don't necessarily jibe with the interests of the individual investor. Journalists aren't looking to maximize returns; they're in the business of attracting attention through their stories. So in addition to straight science reporting (which they tend to do well), biotech journalists at times resemble buy-side analysts; they report on (and thereby promote) trends that are at or near an end for the sake of producing an interesting (and temporarily accurate) story. Or worse still, a journalist will report fairly well on a scientific breakthrough, but readers, lacking a context for the story, overreact in the markets, causing outsized jumps and tumbles in stock prices.

A classic example of investor overreaction to a media story surrounded a May 1999 *New York Times* article about a company called EntreMed. The story focused on the research of Harvard University's

Dr. Judah Folkman, which shed light on the critical role that the formation of new blood vessels plays in the growth of cancers. Folkman's group had discovered two naturally occurring human proteins that inhibited the growth of new blood vessels and effectively stopped the growth of tumors in mice. The article reported that EntreMed, a publicly traded stock, had obtained a license to develop these two proteins as drugs.

The story was very positive toward Folkman's work, featuring quotes that made his discoveries sound even better than they really were. The article ran on the front page on a slow news day in a Sunday edition. EntreMed's stock, which had closed the previous Friday at just over $12 a share, traded as high as $85 the following Monday before closing in the $50s. The stock fell back to earth in 2000, trading as low as $16.125, as doubts arose about the value of Folkman's discoveries as a practical approach to treating cancer. The *Times*-inspired investor who invested in EntreMed was in all likelihood whipsawed, jumping in during or closely after the Monday-in-May frenzy, just in time to ride the stock all the way down.

So biotech's scientists, analysts, and reporters at times inadvertently trigger investor uncertainty and stock price volatility. And the majority of biotech companies, lacking earnings or tangible financial assets, alternately lure and scare off investors. Though both the experts' insights and the companies themselves have value, all of it seems lost in a confused cycle of market fear and greed, played out at the expense of the individual investor in the form of stock price volatility.

Fortunately, there's a way to navigate through biotechnology's many confusions to tap the sector's value. The key is to apply a workable investing philosophy, which in my case is laid out in six rules.

Rule 1—Focus on Long-Term Results

I'm a growth stock investor. When I entered the investment business in 1960, the concept of growth stock investing was relatively new, and I was an early convert. I began by studying companies in technology, the most compelling growth sector at the time. When biotechnology stocks emerged in the late seventies and early eighties, I was immediately attracted to the sector. It didn't take long to appreciate how biotech growth stocks benefited not only from exciting and important new technologies but also from their potential for high profit margins and growth rates and their ability to operate within a proven business model.

Over the next thirty years, I believe the biggest investment opportunities will be in biotechnology growth stocks. In addition to their fundamental appeals, they're also relatively immune to economic cycles, their core businesses are patent-protected, and they're poised to take advantage of favorable demographics over the next thirty to forty years that will increase demand for their products and services.

All that being said, as growth stocks, biotech companies are the furthest thing imaginable from utility stocks. They don't generate steady quarter-to-quarter returns. In the short run, their prices are volatile to the point of being unpredictable.

The key to mitigating the perils of biotech growth stocks is to look past the day-to-day price swings and focus on long-term results. There are two compelling arguments for this approach. The first is that short-term price swings in biotechnology are often the result of the markets behaving emotionally rather than rationally. In the short run, even if the direction of price changes is correct, the magnitude is often exaggerated as a result of the sector's tendency to overreact to the news generated by scientists, analysts, and journalists.

Over time, however, the markets show an uncanny tendency to correct for these overreactions—for example, consider the case of EntreMed, whose stock rose a modest $4 or so across the eighteen months spanning from the day before the *New York Times* story broke to the end of 2000. While the short-term investor would have been elated and then beaten down by the stock's rise and fall, the longer-term investor would have ignored the wild goose chase along the way and focused on the modest return at the end of the ride. The investor taking the short-term view might trust the price information provided by an emotional market and be left utterly confused. The investor taking a longer view might see the workings of a more rational market that eventually returned to fair value.

The second argument for taking the long view in growth stocks is historical. A sizable number of studies and books have been written by such investing notables as Peter Lynch and Burton Malkiel championing the benefits of investing over the long term. Studies examining the viability of the long-term approach over the last eighty years have been particularly well-documented and compelling: Over almost any lengthy subsegment of the past eight decades, common stocks have provided an annual return in the 9 to 10 percent range, better than any other comparable class of investment. The eighty-year period covers an economic depression, several recessions, a world war, a cold war, and other international and domestic mishaps too numerous to mention.

For various lengthy stretches of time across the past fifty years, growth stocks have outperformed common stocks. Over time, the average annual rate of return generated by growth stocks can yield stunning results. Through the magic of compounding, the typical 15 percent long-term growth rate of a drug company (a good proxy for a mature biotech) will turn $10,000 into $662,000 over a thirty-year span. And since over the last thirty years the market has witnessed a general increase in price-earnings ratios, the actual results of many growth stock investors may have substantially exceeded the 15 percent example.

The current market conditions and historical evidence favor the investor who views biotech stocks as I feel they should be regarded, as growth stocks whose long-term prospects more than make up for their short-term inconsistencies. Faith in the long view will enable the individual investor to concentrate on what's important in evaluating these stocks: the strength of the underlying company, based on the quality of its science and the earnings potential for the products it is (or will be) offering. And a focus on the long term will give the individual investor the fortitude to withstand short-run price swings and temporary miscalculations of value by markets acting on emotion.

Rule 2—Invest Rationally, Not Emotionally: Base Decisions on Company Value, Not Fleeting Market Perceptions

Just because growth stocks make great long-term investments does not mean they are going to be the best performers in the market in any given year. In fact, biotech companies have shown a tendency to do very well for a few years, then grow overvalued as too many investors crowd the market and overbid, resulting in a couple of years of relatively poor performance.

The takeaway lesson from this pattern: It is almost as important to buy biotech growth stocks when they are periodically undervalued as it is to own the best-run and most successful companies within the sector. Once invested, the successful biotech investor can focus on the long-term and discount short-term fluctuations. But prior to investing, valuation matters.

In any sector, the classic growth stock investor approach is to research a company, develop a story for why it's going to succeed, invest when its stock is undervalued, and hold it until the stock price is in line with earnings projections or the underlying story changes. This formula applies in biotech as well, but with a few variations.

Short-run pricing in the biotechnology sector is often emotionally driven, both pessimistically and optimistically. During bullish climates, overvaluations of well-run biotech companies can prevent growth investors from buying in for long periods of time. In indifferent or bear markets, undervalued biotech companies may provide growth investors with instant points of entry, but they may also not respond to improving fundamentals for considerable lengths of time. Stock prices can lag behind perceived company valuations for months or even years, trading in narrow ranges until the price moves in tandem with or in anticipation of some event such as a drug approval, important clinical trial results, or the emergence of a favorable corporate partnership, triggering a rapid recovery from long-standing lags in value. The waits to buy in at a good price and for stocks to realize their potential can be very frustrating. Sadly, I have seen many investors give up on stocks just before they move. On the bright side, some of my most successful investments have resulted from buying more of a stock after it has failed to respond quickly to its underlying company's continued progress.

Rule 3—Buy Rationally, Not Emotionally:
If You Believe in a Company, Investing During a
Negative Climate May Be the *Least* Risky Time to Buy

The combination of buying into stocks when they're undervalued and focusing on the long term is the key to success in earning superior returns through growth stock investing. Taking these principles to their extreme in the biotech sector, where short-run prices sometimes fluctuate broadly, leads to a surprising, counterintuitive conclusion: Sometimes the least risky time to invest in a company is when the markets are punishing its stock.

If, based on research, the individual investor believes in the quality of a company that's falling out of favor with the general consensus of the markets, it's a good time to invest. There's a simple reason why this is true: There's a difference between stock price risk and company risk, a distinction that frequently matters a great deal in biotechnology. When academics use the term "risk," they're referring to stock price volatility, but when growth investors use the term, they're thinking of fundamental risk—the risk that the company will be badly managed or go out of business because of excessive competition.

As a sector, biotechnology has more than its share of the academics' version of risk (stock price volatility), but it carries far less fundamental risk. Although there are some inherent business risks unique to biotechnology (the chance that patents won't be approved or drugs won't work in clinical trials, for example), over the years, few biotechnology companies have gone out of business. Certainly, stocks have dropped sharply in the wake of bad news, but many have recovered. The companies whose stocks do not rebound from bad news are often purchased by other biotech companies, thereby salvaging some investor equity. The high survival rate among biotech companies can be attributed largely to the relative lack of competition between products (as a result of patents), as well as the large amount of capital required for drug development, which creates a formidable barrier to entry. These factors afford companies reservoirs of residual value even if the promises of key products never come to fruition.

Amgen, the most successful biotech stock to date, illustrates the difference between stock price risk and company risk. The company began with initial funding from a group of venture capitalists at $4 a share in 1980. When it went public in June 1983, Amgen opened at $18 a share. But late in 1984, despite having five potential drugs in development and a partnership with Abbott Labs to develop DNA probes as diagnostics, Amgen's stock foundered, falling as low as $3.75 per share.

Regardless of the fact that, as a company, Amgen had made steady progress from its inception in 1980 through 1985, the stock experienced drastic fluctuations. MTSL finally recommended Amgen in April 1985 at $5.375 per share, and since that time, this well-managed company has ridden out the short-term emotions of the market to far exceed our expectations for the stock. An investor purchasing one share of Amgen during its IPO would today own forty-eight Amgen shares. And from the time MTSL bought in (1985) to the present, Amgen's market cap has exploded from $60 million to $70 billion.

Despite Amgen's seemingly inexorable rise across the past fifteen years, it's interesting to note that when MTSL decided to invest, the stock was considered risky at less than $6 per share, but at its public offering less than two years prior to this, when Amgen traded at $18, the stock wasn't considered risky at all. The stock may have wavered but the company stayed the course, creating a disparity between price risk and company risk, an ideal situation for a biotechnology growth investor with the right investing philosophy.

Rule 4—Be Patient: Composure Can Increase Returns

In biotechnology, the market timer's luck eventually runs out, whereas the prepared investor is consistently rewarded for patience. One element that attracted me to biotechnology was my conviction that biotech companies react to shifts in investor psychology even more than technology stocks do. The price swings that result from these psychological reactions create excellent opportunities for the prepared individual investor, who often can exploit them more easily than even experienced money managers can. This is because most institutional investors are judged on quarterly performance, an occupational hazard that makes them reluctant to buy even obviously cheap stocks until after they've begun advancing in price. In fact, many buy-side analysts and institutional investors will wait until a stock has doubled in price before making a move. This hesitancy provides a window of opportunity for the individual investor who's willing to buy in and wait a while before the stock price shifts favorably. The individual investor can then enjoy the double benefit of garnering the return the buy-siders miss at the outset and the rapid price movement that often follows when institutional investors finally decide it's safe to jump into the fray.

Another built-in advantage of patience is that it provides a measure of indifference toward irrelevant day-to-day price fluctuations. As long as the fundamentals remain in place, the individual investor doesn't need to constantly track the market—a major advantage in composure over the ever-vigilant institutional investor. Watching and evaluating every nuance brought by each price fluctuation exposes the buy-side analyst and the institutional investor to the perils of fear and greed. It's one of the reasons that stockbrokers tend to be relatively unsuccessful managing their own accounts. The pressure builds, doubt sets in, and they overtrade. I have often asked brokers how they did with a stock we'd discussed months before, only to find they'd sold it after a rather modest move, thereby missing the bulk of the upside. It's a minor tragedy of time horizons and expectations combining to weaken investing resolve, one that the individual investor with a little patience has a good chance of avoiding.

Rule 5—Sell Rationally, Not Emotionally: Don't Wait for the Top Price (Sell When the Market Overvalues the Company)

For many investors, the most difficult part of managing a stock portfolio lies in knowing when to sell. While I pride myself on my ability to buy quality growth stocks when they're out of favor, I almost always agonize over the sell decision. The well-known mantra of the growth stock investor (that is, sell when your reason for buying has disappeared) easily applies to stocks in decline, but the volatile biotech sector sometimes provides a more difficult test for the seller's discipline: Stocks sometimes explode upward.

In biotechnology, the individual investor is occasionally tested by a stock that makes an excessive move up. If it's particularly rapid, it's likely the sign of a moment of market irrationality, and the stock should be sold. For an avid investor, selling at this time may be particularly unpalatable—there may be significant tax consequences, not to mention the nagging doubt that some of the gains will be missed. After all, the only way to identify market highs is to view them in hindsight.

Difficult as it may be, the disciplined investor sells in a hysterically rising market. For a dramatic source of inspiration, one need look back no further than February and March 2000, when most biotech stocks, fueled in part by excitement over genomics, reached crazily high valuation levels, far beyond anything I had anticipated. Unfortunately, I was not immune to their allure; for much of the year, I balanced the call to remain in the market against the call to sell by unloading only a portion of my holdings with each improbable new advance. This worked well for a while, but in a number of cases the stocks moved so much that by the time they reached their highs, I felt foolish for selling some too early. When the heights could not sustain themselves soon after, and I had not fully unwound my positions, I had the opposite emotion—the frustration of having strayed from my investing philosophy.

For the truly aggressive growth stock investor caught in the excitement of a rapidly rising market, there is something to be said for selling part of one's position on the way up, and risking the downturn with the rest. Some investors have had success in selling half of a position after the stock doubles. They find that after they have sold half, the following sell decisions are less emotional and easier to make. For me, it works well to ask if I would be willing to buy the stock at the current price. If the answer is no, I start by selling 20 percent of what I own. I will then sell more if the stock continues to rise. This can be frustrating if the stock's climb continues, as so many did in 2000. I found in 2000 that I was unwilling to sell more at what proved to be the top, because I felt I'd missed out by selling so much at lower prices. In retrospect, that was clearly a mistake.

The need for diversification can also help to force the individual investor to scale out of a position. When a large stock position begins to make a large move, it will soon be too large a part of an investor's total portfolio, making it easier to sell a portion even as the price continues to climb. Often the stock will then correct, and, if it turns out to be a big correction, the investor then has the money to buy back in.

Rule 6—Dare to Be Contrarian: If You're Doing What's Popular at the Time, Worry

This is the catch-all rule in my investing philosophy, and it applies broadly in biotechnology. As I hope I've shown, in this sector— where the scientists aren't always experts, the analysts and journalists have occasional conflicts of interest, the mass of investors is jumpy because most companies don't report earnings, and the markets frequently fail to distinguish between stock price risk and company risk—it pays to be contrarian. The contrarian investor may have to apply a little patience and exert some discipline when buying and selling, but the rewards have been (and I believe will continue to be) there for the taking.

The good news is that the true curmudgeon doesn't have to go it alone; armed with a few techniques, the individual investor can work through the conflicts of industry experts to glean real value from the information they provide. And as I mentioned earlier, there are fairly effective proxies that can substitute for earnings in companies that have yet to turn a profit. By working through the mechanics of growth stock investing while keeping the rest of my investing rules in mind, I find it easier to maintain my position as a contrarian and pursue better returns than I might otherwise see by following the unpredictable, ever-changing conventional wisdom of the markets.

A Quick Summary

Focus on the long term, make rational investing and purchasing decisions, be patient, sell rationally, and aspire to be contrarian—my six rules (my investing philosophy) in a nutshell. They fit my outlook as an aggressive growth stock investor, and I feel they work particularly well in the biotech sector. Your own investing psychology may differ somewhat from mine—you may be more risk averse, for example. The most important lesson is to build a set of rules that can give you the resolve to act consistently and effectively in the wide variety of market conditions that biotechnology often presents. Once you have your own working version of an investing philosophy, stick with it; work your way through the mechanics of investing with it in mind, and you'll make better decisions in the marketplace.

CHAPTER 5

The Cutting Edge of Biotech: Disease Treatments

Regardless of whether we hold shares in biotech stocks, every person living today has a stake in the biotech industry. As the industry seeks to fulfill its mission of improving living conditions worldwide, it pursues cutting-edge developments that will shape everyone's future through improvements in health, food supply, products, and overall quality of life. Its biggest efforts, of course, have gone toward alleviating human suffering from disease—biotech aggressively targets every disease, from rare conditions afflicting only a few thousand people to the most common causes of death.

Learning something about these diseases and their sufferers is a useful point of entry for investors. To evaluate a company and its pipeline of drugs in development, investors need to consider both the potential market for a drug (this chapter takes a first look) as well as how long it will take the drug to gain marketing approval (a later chapter covers this in detail). Every disease is unique, bringing biotech companies unique challenges as they work to develop suitable drugs. With these challenges come unique opportunities.

Current developments in biotech will have enormous impact. Of the approximately 200 products now in late-stage clinical trials, at least 30 have the potential to generate sales in excess of a billion dollars. New drugs to treat cardiovascular disease can help as much as 20 percent of the population of the United States. And the next five to ten years will bring dramatic changes in cancer treatments, resulting in more people living with the disease than dying from it.

These two primary killers, cardiovascular disease and cancer, along with the other most prevalent categories of disease, inflammatory and autoimmune diseases, metabolic diseases and hormones, and brain and nervous system diseases, account for most of the drugs biotech companies currently have in development. While learning about rare diseases may help a biotech investor evaluate a niche drug, examining these five main categories will cover most of the current and upcoming big opportunities.

Cardiovascular Disease

Cardiovascular disease—diseases of the heart and circulatory system—is the leading cause of death in the United States, killing one million people a year. The number of Americans suffering from some form of the disease, currently 58 million, is increasing. This rise is fed by two factors: Improved treatments have prolonged patients' lives, turning what were once death statistics into disease statistics; and a population bulging toward older age puts a larger number of people in the disease's path. In fact, the main culprit in cardiovascular disease—a hardening of the arteries known as atherosclerosis—is part of the body's natural aging process.

In atherosclerosis, cholesterol, clotting substances, and smooth muscle cells conspire to form plaque, which builds up inside the blood vessels and reduces blood flow. This raises blood pressure and puts one at risk for a more serious condition should the plaque break off—in an attempt to repair the damage, the body will form a blood clot, which can stop blood flow. In the coronary arteries, this means a heart attack. In the arteries leading to the brain, it means a stroke. If the clot migrates to the lungs, it can cause a pulmonary embolism. Each of these events is life threatening.

To physicians, treating cardiovascular disease breaks down to two stages of care: managing chronic (or ongoing) conditions such as high cholesterol and high blood pressure and handling acute (or emergency) events such as heart attack or stroke. Each stage requires an array of drugs, and chronic conditions typically require daily medications. Looking at cardiovascular disease's sizable and growing market, the need for multiple drugs, the presence of emergency and long-term prescription patients, and the usual barriers to entry provided by patent protection, we see one of the largest and most hotly contested markets in biotechnology.

New drugs with new approaches can soar. For years, physicians tried to treat chronic cardiovascular disease in one of two ways: by lowering blood pressure (using calcium channel blockers and ace inhibitors) or by reducing the heart rate (using beta blockers). Accordingly, most large drug companies have long marketed and realized considerable profits from these treatments. Recently, however, a new category of cardiovascular drugs has surpassed the industry mainstays. Statins, which lower cholesterol levels, now claim worldwide sales of $20 billion. Pfizer's Lipitor is the market's top seller.

Biotech has certainly helped medicine take strides in the treatment of chronic cardiovascular conditions, but it has taken bigger steps in acute care. Early on, Genentech developed Activase, which improved the body's ability to break up blood clots and limit the damage from heart attacks. The company followed up with TNKase, a second-generation product to dissolve blood clots that is much easier to administer. Other biotech companies have developed drugs that keep the body from forming blood clots in the first place. These drugs, called GPIIb/IIIa inhibitors, were first approved for use in conjunction with angioplasty procedures (which open narrowed vessels), but physicians now employ them to treat patients who present at hospitals with heart pain but no heart attack. Centocor (since acquired by Johnson & Johnson) pioneered these drugs with a monoclonal antibody in late 1994 only to be overtaken by Merck and Cor Therapeutics, now a subsidiary of Millennium, when they introduced products at a cheaper price point. Over half the patients in this market now use Cor Therapeutics' Integrilin. Tests of these two types of drugs—blood clot dissolvers such as TNKase and anti-clotting drugs such as Integrilin—in combination have shown promising results as well.

Biotech companies are also making headway in developing drugs to treat congestive heart failure, a condition where the heart fails to circulate or pump blood adequately. With few effective treatments available, this area offers substantial market opportunity, especially as improvements in critical care increase the number of patients with injured hearts who survive. The first approval of a drug in this category, for Scios' Natecor, a naturally occurring human protein,

came in mid-2001. It may not be a smooth path—Natecor's early results were disappointing—but biotech's near future will include
more approvals for drugs that treat congestive heart failure.

Regardless of the stage of treatment, sales of new cardiovascular
drugs typically grow slowly. Charged with the management of life-
threatening ailments, cardiologists are understandably cautious when
considering new treatments. This conservatism creates a window for
investors, who may be able to buy the stock of a company with an approved drug at a reasonable price. Over the years, we've recommended a few such opportunities in the *Medical Technology Stock Letter*.
Cor Therapeutics, for example, still had a market capitalization of only
$330 million in July 1998, even after Integrilin (Cor's anticlotting
drug) had gained approval. More recently, in March 2001, the
Medicines Company had a total market capitalization of $317 million
following the approval of its first drug. Both investments proved favorable, and Cor has tripled since the recommendation.

Cancer

Although cardiovascular disease takes far more lives than cancer,
the second largest cause of death in the United States, more biotech
drugs in development target cancer than any other disease, partly
due to the more favorable regulations for cancer drugs. Roughly 40
percent of the drugs currently in clinical trials aim to treat cancer or
reduce the side effects of cancer treatments.

Because so much of biotech's work concerns cancer, and because
the disease itself manifests in so many different ways, it's worth taking a more in-depth look at the historical treatments of cancer along
with the current approaches. By gaining a foothold in understanding biotech's massive effort against cancer, investors may identify
many attractive investment opportunities.

Cancer is usually thought of as a single disease, when in fact it
encompasses more than 200 different diseases as classified by the
medical community and cancer researchers. Historically, cancers
have been identified by the part of the body from which they origi-
nate, but this method is inadequate, as a single body part can develop different cancers with vastly different characteristics. For example, there are several types of skin cancer, ranging from the fairly

common, relatively benign basal cell carcinoma to the rarer, life-threatening melanoma. Lung cancers can appear as either small-cell lung cancer or non-small-cell lung cancer, which respond to treatments differently. Most general discussions, however, refer to cancer as a whole.

In cancer, cells grow out of control and form tumors, most commonly in the major organs, though cancer can also develop in the lymph system, muscles, bones, bone marrow, or other areas of the body. Tumors invade healthy body tissue and, if untreated, metastasize, or spread, to other parts of the body. Although the causes of cancer are not fully understood, scientists have found correlations between particular cancers and environmental or hereditary risk factors: Smoking is the main cause of lung cancer; family history appears to play a large role in breast cancer.

The conventional treatments for cancer are surgery, radiation therapy, and chemotherapy (chemotherapy is where biotechnology mostly comes in). Upon their widespread adoption in the mid-twentieth century, these treatments greatly improved the outlook for many types of cancers, although they made little difference in others. Often, physicians use these three modes of treatment in combination for more effective results. Surgery to excise the tumor may be followed by radiation therapy, which destroys abnormal cells with a directed X-ray or other source of radioactivity, or chemotherapy, in which cancer-killing drugs are typically administered intravenously. Chemotherapy drugs may also be used in combination with each other. Essentially, most chemotherapy drugs are selective poisons that act on the body's most rapidly dividing cells. This means that, in addition to cancer cells, they attack the cells of the stomach lining, blood, and hair follicles, bringing the common side effects of nausea, anemia, and hair loss.

Since President Nixon declared a "war on cancer" in 1971, increased spending on cancer research has brought advances in scientific understanding of the disease. (The practical results, however, have taken longer than people expected, which is par for the course in basic research.) Scientists now know, for instance, that for many different types of cancer the same molecular changes are implicated in turning healthy cells into cancer cells. These changes can occur inside the cell or on the cell surface. Inside the cell, mutations in genes that control cell growth can trigger cancer. On the cell surface, overexpression of a receptor for one of the growth factors sets the stage for cancer. Pinpointing these changes meant identifying new targets for the development of anticancer drugs. This and other developments in molecular biology and biotech put us on the verge of breakthroughs for cancer treatments.

Worldwide, the market for cancer drugs now tops $10 billion. Individual drugs can claim huge pieces of this market. Bristol-Myers Squibb's Taxol, the most successful chemotherapy drug, gained approval in 1992 and grew annual sales to reach more than $1.6 billion before generic competition appeared in 2000. IDEC Pharmaceuticals' Rituxan, a monoclonal antibody to treat non-Hodgkin's lymphoma that the company comarkets with Genentech, debuted in 1997 and reached U.S. sales of $779 million in 2001. And Genentech's Herceptin, a monoclonal antibody that targets breast cancer, holds the record for first-year sales of a cancer drug with $184 million in 1999, a figure that climbed to $347 million in 2001.

The market for cancer drugs will only get bigger. Just as with cardiovascular disease, cancer risk increases as people grow older, so the aging of the population will bring more cases every year. Also, as cancer drugs continue to improve, they will replace many forms of treatment currently in use.

Nixon's call for a "war" was only mildly hyperbolic. On the front lines, physicians seize everything available to them to combat cancer, often prescribing chemotherapy combinations that include drugs not yet approved for the particular type of cancer they're treating. Biotech companies are attacking cancer from every imaginable angle, pursuing such approaches as immunotherapy, cell surface receptors, antiangiogenesis, genetic mutation treatments, and hormone-based treatments, as well as combinations of two or more of these.

Immunotherapy

In immunotherapy, an introduced agent stimulates the body's immune system to attack the targeted disease. Biotech's first contribution to cancer treatment came in immunotherapy, when companies tried to use signaling molecules, called cytokines, to launch the body's attack on the disease. These cytokines have not been particularly successful in treating cancer, despite the big names behind them—Chiron markets interleukin 2 (IL–2) as Proleukin, and Schering-Plough (under license from Biogen) and Hoffmann–La Roche (under license from Genentech) market alpha interferon. Currently, large injections must be administered frequently to maintain an effective drug level, and the high doses cause too many significant side effects.

One way around the cytokines' limitations is to change the delivery method, an approach a number of biotech companies are pursuing. Gene therapy, the insertion of altered genes into cells, could direct continuous release of cytokines near the cancer, focusing the immune stimulation and reducing side effects. The gene therapy company Valentis is working with Hoffmann–La Roche on products to deliver IL–2 and IL–12 to treat a number of different types of cancer. If approved, these could be the first gene therapy products, reaching the market within the next two or three years.

Another company, Cell Genesys, has developed a gene therapy to deliver the cytokine granulocyte-macrophage colony stimulating factor (GM-CSF) that has shown encouraging preliminary results in treating prostate and lung cancer and will enter final testing in mid-2002. Immunex's Leukine also uses GM-CSF in its protein form to restore levels of white blood cells after chemotherapy.

Cancer vaccines offer another approach to immunotherapy. Unlike commonly known vaccines, which prevent a particular disease, cancer vaccines do not prevent cancer, but treat it. By stimulating a response against cancer cells specifically, cancer vaccines promise the advantage of a long-lasting benefit from only a few injections, with minimal side effects. Currently, companies are pursuing two different options for developing these vaccines—introducing cancer-specific antigens combined with an immune stimulant or removing, modifying, and reinserting the patient's own cancer cells. Development remains slow, but overall cancer vaccines have great long-term potential.

Cell Surface Receptors

As mentioned earlier, the overexpression of a receptor for a growth factor on the surface of a cell can set the stage for many cancers. When growth factors subsequently activate these receptors, the receptors send a signal to the cell, telling it to divide at the accelerated pace that is characteristic of cancer. Stopping this growth stops the cancer, so cell surface receptors make excellent targets for cancer drugs.

Monoclonal antibodies that block these receptors have slowed cancer growth and, in some cases, even reduced the size of cancers. The first of these products, Genentech's Herceptin, targets the HER–2 receptor, which is overexpressed on a third of breast cancers and some other cancers, and has achieved great market success. The next product likely to gain approval is ImClone Systems' Erbitux, which blocks the epidermal growth factor (EGF) receptor. The EGF receptor is overexpressed on no less than half of all solid tumors, including nearly all head and neck cancers. Given that the EGF receptor overexpresses in at least five times as many cancers as the HER–2 receptor, ImClone has an incredible opportunity here. To help capitalize on it, ImClone entered into a partnership with Bristol-Myers Squibb in September 2001, gaining not only cash payments of $1 billion but also the services of the largest oncology sales force in the United States.

So far, test results for ImClone's Erbitux have been promising in combination with radiation and other chemotherapies, but modest for its use alone. By themselves, monoclonal antibodies are not very effective at killing cancer cells—they simply stop the cells from growing further. Biotech companies have put a lot of effort into finding a way to attach a killing agent to the monoclonal antibody, experimenting with radioactive isotopes and potent toxins. The first monoclonal antibody with a radioactive isotope (IDEC's Zevalin) will reach the market in 2002, with Corxia's Bexxar right behind it. Work with toxins has brought mostly disappointment, but one company, ImmunoGen, after many failures, has developed a method of attaching a potent toxin that suppresses its toxicity until it enters the cancer cell. With two products showing favorable early results, ImmunoGen has signed a number of impressive licensing agreements that allow other companies to use the ImmunoGen toxin with their own monoclonal antibodies. Licensees include such monoclonal antibody leaders as Genentech and Abgenix.

Besides blocking the receptor itself, another approach to preventing cancer growth caused by overexpression of cell surface receptors is to interfere with the signal sent by the receptor. A number of companies, including OSI Pharmaceuticals, Pfizer, Astra-Zeneca, and Pharmacia, have active projects that use small molecule drugs to inhibit tyrosine kinase, a key enzyme in the signaling pathway, thus stopping the growth signal. Concerns about side effects arise here, as similar tyrosine kinases also control other enzymes in the body.

Antiangiogenesis

As cancer tumors grow, they need new blood vessels to provide the oxygen and nutriments necessary for further growth. While this concept may seem obvious now, it met with great skepticism when Judah Folkman first advanced it at Harvard in the 1970s. Since then, it has generated an entire area of research for cancer treatment—antiangiogenesis, or preventing (anti) the blood vessels (angio) from undergoing new growth (genesis).

At least a dozen companies are developing antiangiogenesis agents. EntreMed, by no means the furthest along, has nonetheless received the most publicity, primarily because it has the rights to two signaling proteins discovered by Folkman's lab in the mid-1990s. EntreMed has seen results using these proteins in mice, but it is still in early-stage trials with humans and has encountered some trouble making the proteins. The company is also working with Cell Genesys to deliver these proteins using gene therapy.

Both Chiron and Celera are pursuing antiangiogenesis by working to block another protein that is active in the formation of new blood vessels, urokinase. Still more companies have focused on vascular endothelial growth factor (VEGF), one of the prime signals that instructs the body to grow new blood vessels. Genentech is conducting clinical trials with a protein that attaches to and inactivates VEGF; ImClone Systems is developing a monoclonal antibody that blocks the VEGF receptor; and Chiron, in partnership with Ribozyme, is testing a modified ribozyme (naturally occurring pieces of genetic material that act as enzymes) that blocks the production of the VEGF receptor.

These antiangiogenesis efforts have yet to show conclusive results in humans, but I am optimistic that one or more will prove effective. I foresee them working particularly well in combination therapy.

Genetic Mutation Treatments

Directly treating the genetic mutation that causes a cancer is another option in cancer treatment. Recent gains in understanding the genetic mutations that cause particular cancers have made it possible to design therapies that deal with these changes. If the mutation involves the production of a protein that makes a cell grow, antisense or a ribozyme can stop that production. If the mutation involves the lack of a protein that should control the cell cycle, gene therapy can replace this protein. Controlling or taking advantage of mutations holds huge long-term potential, but few treatments have been tested extensively in humans.

With so many mutations that produce too much of a specific protein implicated in cancer, there are a number of excellent targets for antisense, which can block the production of a protein. Further, antisense's ability to be very specific makes it a good candidate for developing treatments with few side effects. Quite a few companies are working on antisense treatments, including Isis, the antisense leader, which has several anticancer drugs in development. Isis's most advanced product, a PKC-alpha inhibitor to treat non-small-cell lung cancer in combination with chemotherapy, has moved into final-stage testing after showing very impressive results in earlier trials. Genta has taken its bcl–2 inhibitor, which prevents cell death, to final-stage testing for the treatment of melanoma, and AVI Biosciences is conducting preclinical studies on potential antisense cancer treatments.

As for gene therapy to replace the lack of a protein that should control the cell cycle, the gene most often involved is the p53 gene. The p53 gene is part of a pathway that prevents cells with other mutations from dividing. About half of all cancers have a malfunctioning p53 gene. Introgen has entered final-stage testing with a p53 gene therapy after earlier work showed that successful insertion of the p53 gene into cancer cells caused the cells to stop dividing and then die. Making this intriguing concept work with human patients in large clinical trials may be a challenge, however.

Onyx Pharmaceuticals is taking another approach involving the p53 gene, harnessing a virus associated with the common cold, the adenovirus, to kill cancer cells. Normally, the adenovirus turns off the p53 gene in order to replicate itself in human cells. Onyx has selected the adenovirus, removing its ability to block the p53 gene so that it can thereafter only replicate in cells that have a malfunctioning p53 gene. When injected into such cancer cells in tests, the adenovirus replicated, attacked nearby cancer cells, and killed many of them. In partnership with Pfizer, Onyx is conducting final-stage tests of this approach for treatment of head and neck cancer. The company is targeting other types of cancer as well and is also pursuing the possibility of administering the treatment by infusion into the bloodstream rather than by injection directly into the cancer. If successful, infusion would allow the treatment of cancers that have spread to other sites.

Hormone-Based Treatments

Some human cancers, most notably breast and prostate cancers, need hormones to continue to grow. Therefore, stopping the production of the hormones may constitute effective treatment of these cancers. In many breast cancers, the culpable hormone is estrogen; similarly, prostate cancer depends on testosterone for growth. The drugs of choice here are tamoxifen to block the production of estrogen and leupolide to depress testosterone (usually after surgery that removes the prostate tumor).

Much of the current development in hormone-based treatments focuses on delivery methods. A couple of extended-release forms of leupolide are now on the market, and others are under development. Further understanding of the multiple roles of the sex-related hormones may bring better treatments, such as compounds that selectively block those hormones' receptors on cancer cells. Ligand Pharmaceuticals leads this area of research.

Despite this wealth of promising approaches, we should keep our expectations in check, as cancer brings substantial clinical challenges. New treatments are usually first approved as rescue therapies for patients who have failed existing treatments (despite the fact that they may be most effective in newly diagnosed patients). Only once additional trials have shown success in early-stage patients will new treatments earn wider approvals. Then they must go through yet more clinical work to determine their role in potential combination therapies. Outside of rescue therapies, inherently conservative physicians may balk at adopting new therapies without long-term data.

Inflammatory and Autoimmune Diseases

While inflammation plays a critical role in protecting the body, it can be dangerous in excessive amounts. Excessive inflammation forms the root of inflammation disorders, and it is the primary symptom of autoimmune diseases such as lupus or rheumatoid arthritis, in which the immune system attacks the body itself. In terms of drug development, inflammatory and autoimmune diseases have been grouped together as a single target for research, creating a sizable market for the industry.

Essentially, inflammation occurs as the body responds to damage from either microbes or physical injury by increasing blood flow to the injured area, and associated fluid increases and nerve stimulation cause swelling and pain. The details of the inflammation process, however, are extremely complicated. The entire inflammation process is best described as a cascade, a succession of stages where each stage acts on the product of the preceding stage.

To understand how to fight inflammation, scientists have been drawn to the immune system, of which inflammation is a part. Unfortunately, the more they learn, the more they still don't understand. The complexity of the human immune system has brought difficulties and disappointments to biotech companies working to develop anti-inflammatory products, but it also allows them to go after a number of different points for intervention. Scientists have moved beyond white blood cell growth stimulants (such as Amgen's Neupogen, still a powerhouse product), focusing instead on interleukins and interferons (types of immune system signaling molecules). These have yielded successful approved products—alpha interferon, which stimulates the immune system in the treatment of some cancers and hepatitis; IL–2, which also uses stimulation to treat various types of cancer; and beta interferon, which turns down the immune system response to stop the progression of multiple sclerosis. More recently, scientists have begun to understand the complement system, which operates early in the immune response, making it a prime target for inhibiting the complex cascade that leads to inflammation. Avant Therapeutics and Alexion both have drugs in development that take this approach.

Biotechnology companies' work on developing treatments for the most prevalent autoimmune/inflammatory diseases—rheumatoid arthritis, sepsis or septic shock, inflammatory bowel disease, and psoriasis—yields benefits (and opens the doors to secondary markets) beyond these ailments as well. For example, as we learn more about inflammation, we also find that it plays a key role in other medical problems, such as reperfusion injury, which occurs in the heart or brain after the blood supply has been cut off by some trauma and then restored.

Ultimately, the winners in finding effective treatments for inflammation are likely to be the biotech companies that have made it a primary focus. Not all of the drugs they work to develop will prove successful, but each effort will provide them with more knowledge and increase their chances of later getting it right. Immunex, for example, has benefited from its long history of studying the various human proteins involved in the inflammation process in its development of Enbrel, a drug that targets tumor necrosis factor (or TNF, an inflammatory molecule found in large amounts at the site of many inflammations). In 1988, Enbrel was approved for the treatment of moderate to severe rheumatoid arthritis that had failed to respond to other existing treatments. Later, Enbrel gained approval for the treatment of other forms of rheumatoid arthritis. In 2001, Enbrel sales reached $762 million and would have kept climbing if not for manufacturing capacity limitations.

Immunex's Enbrel may face its strongest competition not as a result of superior science, but rather as a result of superior delivery. All of the TNF drugs on the market currently require injection, so any company that could offer a pill-form TNF inhibitor would have a major market advantage. Both ICOS and Isis Pharmaceuticals have recently begun testing versions of such a drug on humans. ICOS is especially worth watching here, as it distinguishes itself by its practice of testing potential drugs in a number of diseases—a system that cofounder and former CEO George Rathmann brought from his experience at Amgen.

In addition to a pill-form TNF inhibitor, ICOS has many other inflammation programs under way. The one perhaps closest to fruition is Pafase, which targets one of the most significant proinflammatory mediators and has shown promise in treating the symptoms of severe sepsis, an acute bacterial infection of the blood. Final-stage clinical trials, initiated in 2001, will determine the drug's potential in this large market.

Sepsis remains one of the greatest challenges for biotech companies targeting inflammatory disease. About 500,000 cases of sepsis (which can progress to septicemia or septic shock) occur each year, usually in hospitals, and the death rate is around 40 percent. Although physicians can treat the infection with antibiotics, the immune system overreaction often continues, injuring the lungs, liver, or other major organs. Attempts to treat sepsis have brought biotech companies several spectacular failures—testing the drugs has proven difficult, as the disease afflicts such a great variety of patients. Cancer patients with immune systems weakened by chemotherapy or radiation may respond very differently than otherwise healthy trauma patients suffering severe blood loss.

The biotech industry has tried a number of approaches in developing drugs to treat sepsis. The first attempts featured monoclonal antibodies, and other notable attempts included the use of various proteins to mimic the body's own process of controlling excessive inflammation. Following earlier failures by Xoma and Centocor, Synergen (since acquired by Amgen) and Chiron have both carried sepsis drugs into final-stage testing, but so far all of these efforts have failed as well.

Much remains on the horizon for inflammatory and autoimmune disease treatment. Opportunities abound for biotech companies, both in addressing symptoms and delivery options. I expect a number of new blockbuster drugs to emerge over the next five years to reach these large potential markets.

Metabolic Disease and Hormones

Hormones and the regulation of the body's growth and metabolism play critical roles in human health. Consequently, disorders involving these factors often provide large targets for biotech companies. As biotechnology's understanding of hormones continues to rapidly increase, the industry will generate more and more products for this area.

The debut of the first hormone product in 1985, Genentech's human growth hormone (HGH), represents one of biotech's earliest accomplishments. Since then, the industry has been looking for uses of HGH beyond preventing dwarfism in infants and children lacking adequate production of the hormone. Considerable work and speculation have centered on the importance of HGH in wound healing, its potential for treating wasting associated with AIDS (as approved), and its possible use in managing some of the effects of aging. I remember reading about an Eli Lilly study where twenty-one men between the ages of fifty-five and sixty-five who took HGH not only showed significant increases in lean body mass, but actually looked and felt younger. Lilly didn't pursue a larger study, however, as it realized that it would encounter enormous complications in gaining approval to market HGH to slow aging, since from a Food and Drug Administration perspective, aging is not a disease. To prove that the benefits outweighed any potential risks, Lilly would have to complete a large, lengthy clinical trial, treating thousands of people for ten or more years—a very costly proposition that might deliver results just as most protection from competition expired, removing much of the profit potential.

In addition to HGH, a number of biotech companies have pursued the use of another, related hormone, insulinlike growth factor (IGF). In studies, IGF has shown promise in wound healing and bone growth, making it suitable for treating conditions ranging from type-II diabetes to hip fractures. Both Genentech and Chiron have conducted testing of IGF's ability to treat a number of different diseases, but have yet to gain approval for any IGF-related drug. Chiron came close in a partnership project with Cephalon that targeted amyotrophic lateral sclerosis (ALS, often referred to as Lou Gehrig's disease) and showed positive results in European but not U.S. trials. One of the obstacles with IGF is dosages—large dosages overcome the body's response of quickly clearing IGF from the bloodstream, but they also cause more side effects. A small biotech company, Insmed, may have resolved this issue by using IGF in combination with its binding protein, causing it to circulate in the bloodstream in its normal form until the body activates it when and where it is needed. So far, Insmed's tests have shown positive results.

Perhaps the most obvious market for hormone drugs is replacement therapy for the sexual hormones testosterone and estrogen. For years, men have used testosterone to compensate for deficient natural production or as their own production diminishes with aging, and many women take estrogen after menopause to reduce the dangers of osteoporosis and heart attack. Here, delivery methods will help determine the winners. The current prevailing methods such as daily pills may be supplanted by new delivery systems such as transdermals (skin patches and ointments), poised to hit the market soon.

Again, side effects are an issue. Estrogen, for instance, has been linked to increased incidence of breast cancer. But as scientists learn more about these hormones, they are finding better solutions. The discovery that estrogen interacts with different cell receptors in different parts of the body led to the design of small molecule drugs that act much like estrogen, but activate only the desired receptors. Eli Lilly's Evista, approved to treat osteoporosis, was the first of these selective estrogen receptor modulators (SERMs). Both Pfizer and American Home Products are conducting late-stage clinical trials of second-generation SERMs using technology licensed from the biotech company Ligand Pharmaceuticals, the leader in this area. These products show the potential for treating osteoporosis and reducing heart attack risk in women with no side effects and point to similar possibilities for selective activation of the receptors that respond to androgen (a male hormone) in men, which Ligand is also exploring.

Brain and Nervous System Diseases

Of all the diseases for which biotech companies have sought to develop treatments, diseases of the brain and nervous system have brought the most mixed results. Large pharmaceutical companies have made fortunes supplying the vast markets for anxiety, depression, and pain—Hoffmann–La Roche's initial success came largely from sales of Valium and Xanax to treat anxiety, and Eli Lilly saw more than $2 billion in sales annually with its leading second-generation treatment for depression, Prozac (which went off patent in 2001). Yet no effective treatments exist for some of the world's most heartbreaking disorders, including Alzheimer's disease (which afflicts 4 million Americans), Parkinson's disease, and ALS.

Furthermore, because of characteristics unique to the brain and nervous system, solutions for these diseases appear to be a long way off. To begin with, scientists know less about the brain than any other organ. They cannot observe its operation outside the body and they cannot draw many parallels from animal studies, because human brain characteristics are both unique and astonishingly complex. The brain is regulated by electronic impulses fired across trillions of synapses between billions of dendrites stemming from 10 billion neurons, which—unlike other cells in the body that constantly cycle through death and replacement—do not reproduce.

Beyond the enduring mysteries of its structure, the brain's mechanics pose another formidable challenge to drug developers. A membrane called the blood-brain barrier prevents large proteins and potentially harmful substances from reaching the neurons within the brain. While this helps keep the brain safe, it also creates a huge obstacle in drug development, since it prevents many potential treatments from ever reaching the brain.

In recent years, two new groups of companies have formed to pursue opportunities in brain and nervous system research. The first group uses the latest advances in neuroscience to design more specific drugs to treat the established markets for anxiety, depression, and pain. The second group focuses on the challenges of neurodegenerative diseases, researching proteins that help keep neurons alive and functioning properly, called neurotrophic factors.

To date, treatments involving neurotrophic factors have shown only modest success in clinical trials. Not only do neurotrophic factors have difficulty passing through the blood-brain barrier, but the fact that the various factors work in concert with one another also makes it harder to demonstrate results when testing them one at a time. Still, the area's enormous potential is appealing. Beyond instilling hope for future treatments of the most prevalent brain and nervous system diseases, neurotrophic factors can be used to treat peripheral nervous system diseases such as motor neuron diseases and peripheral neuropathy, where the affected neurons are outside the brain and thus more accessible.

Looking Further

While by no means an exhaustive list of the industry's activities, the heart of the biotech sector is in cardiovascular disease, cancer, inflammatory and autoimmune diseases, metabolic diseases, hormones, and diseases of the brain and nervous system. These areas of inquiry encompass most of the sizable opportunities that currently exist.

To the individual investor, the specifics of biotech companies' work on these diseases may seem complex and difficult. But by keeping in mind the diseases themselves, investors can begin to evaluate biotech companies from more familiar territory. On a personal level, most investors have seen these diseases affect someone they know. Based on that background, even a modest understanding of how a potential treatment could help patients can give investors a good sense of direction for finding further information (company web sites are a good start). From this angle, investors can see biotech companies not as a bewildering, foreign landscape, but as relevant, vital opportunities.

CHAPTER 6

The Cutting Edge of Biotech: Genomics

When scientists finished sequencing the entire human genome in 2000, genomics became biotech's biggest story. Even though most people didn't wholly grasp the importance of the achievement, the concept of a fully mapped-out human genome seemed to excite everyone. After years of work, science had a complete, accurate map of every segment of DNA that makes up every gene within the set of twenty-three chromosomes that encode all the aspects of the human body, including the traits that distinguish and unite all of us. To put it in grand terms, the mapping of the human genome is a landmark in the history of man's pursuit of self-knowledge. The achievement in itself is inherently fascinating, but the media added intrigue to the story in 2000 by publicizing a subplot: the race to finish the sequencing, pitting the Human Genome Project, an international cooperative effort (whose contribution in this country was funded by the U.S. government) against Celera, a publicly traded company.

As a result, the mapping of the genome turned into a great yarn, capturing the public's attention and generating a lot of excitement among investors. The investors' enthusiasm translated into large moves in the stock prices of biotech's newcomers, the genomics companies. Celera, having gone public in mid-1999, rose from $20 to a high of $276 between September 1999 and February 25, 2000 (adjusting for stock splits). Across the next nineteen months, Celera's stock worked its way downward once again, reaching a low of $19 on

September 21, 2001. Another company working on sequencing, Human Genome Sciences, matched Celera's late 1999 rise, ballooning from $18 at the end of September 1999 to $116 on March 1, 2000, before sliding down to a low of $26 on September 27, 2001.

The sharp movements of the stocks of Celera and Human Genome Sciences illustrate a key point of practical biotech investing: In this sector, getting excited about the science can be dangerous for the investor. The mapping of the genome remains a groundbreaking achievement, and genomics will have a widespread impact on the biotech industry across the next twenty years. It doesn't follow from either of these facts, however, that we can confidently envision the future of genomics. Certainly there are some early developments that can inform the individual investor's thinking, but the broader truth remains: As exciting as genomic's future is, no one yet knows which companies will benefit the most.

What Is Genomics?

Genomics is the investigation of genes. Although the emphasis is on human genes, much has also been learned by studying the genes of other organisms, including mice, zebra fish, fruit flies, yeast, and bacteria. As in humans, the genomes of these organisms are composed of a common, stable structure, pairs of nucleotide bases (adenine with thiamine and cytosine with guanine) organized in a double-helix pattern to form DNA (deoxyribonucleic acid). This fundamental similarity, shared by all genomes, has enabled scientists to identify the function of specific genes—coded by a particular section of DNA—in one organism and then look for similar genes in humans.

Now with the completion of the sequencing of the 3 million base pairs that make up the human genome, the real work of genomics is about to commence. The focus now shifts to exploring the functions of specific genes and discovering how different genes interact with one another. As impressive an accomplishment as mapping the genome is, it's yet another example of a discovery that only leads to more questions. Completing the human genome isn't an end; it's a beginning.

In some ways, it's been a bumpy beginning for genomics. The recent confusion surrounding the true number of human genes illustrates how much more there is to learn. Before the sequence of the genome was complete, the estimates for the total number of human genes ranged from roughly 30,000 to well in excess of 100,000. As a biotech enthusiast, I'd been fascinated by these guesses for several years, and my early inclination was to assume that the higher estimates were closer to the mark. However, the "correct" answer turned out to be more complicated than I (or perhaps anyone) might have guessed.

The emergence of wide gaps between the high and low estimates grew out of semantics, not science. Different parties had different definitions for a gene. The low estimates came from scientists looking at the human genome sequence and identifying what they considered to be separate genes. This approach may seem sensible and straightforward to the layperson, but historically much of the work on identifying genes has relied on a different method, one that produced much higher estimates for the number of human genes.

The scientists making the higher estimates were looking for active genes, which led them to separate all of the messenger RNA (ribonucleic acid) within a cell. (Messenger RNA, formed by the cell when a particular gene is activated, is a reverse copy of DNA that serves as a template for making the amino acids chains that form the proteins for which the gene is coded.) Since messenger RNA degrades easily, these scientists copied it as complementary DNA. In their resulting libraries of complementary DNA, they looked for specific genes. Because the physical genes noted in the sequencing of a stretch of the genome can code for more than one protein, and because each protein is coded for by a specific complementary DNA, companies such as Incyte Genomics (which used the complementary DNA method) arrived at much higher estimates for the number of human genes. This functional information is what is useful for identifying targets for new drugs.

While I think the key number is the sum of proteins that are uniquely produced directly by human genes (around 150,000), for investing purposes, it isn't necessary to settle on a final gene tally. It's not even necessary to agree on the definition of a gene. It is worth noting, however, that the term means different things to different scientists, and that as genomics gets off the ground, even the most basic terminology is ground for debate.

What's Next: Functional Genomics

Putting semantics aside, now that the human genome has been sequenced, the challenge is to find ways to use the information to make new drugs. In most cases, the first step in this process is to determine what the newly discovered genes do. Speaking practically, this means identifying what protein the gene instructs the cell to produce, then learning the function the protein performs within the body. The pursuit of these questions is most often referred to as functional genomics, or target validation.

Though it's still a fairly new area of inquiry, functional genomics already features a series of techniques for uncovering the purpose of individual genes. I believe that these methods, which include comparing genes, using "knockout" mice, and using antisense techniques, will end up complementing rather than competing with each other as scientists use every tool at their disposal to learn the secrets of the genome.

The first of these methods, comparing genes, means comparing the sequence of the gene with that of similar genes whose functions are already understood. The idea is that if the genes are similar, the proteins produced by the genes may have similar functions within the body. With tens of thousands of genes and some 3 million base pairs to be analyzed, bioinformatics (sophisticated software for harnessing the huge amount of data being created) is becoming indispensable to the process of making these identifications and comparisons.

Another way of determining a gene's functions is to delete the gene in another organism, usually a mouse, and then make observations and perform tests. The single-gene-deleted "knockout" mice can be very helpful in defining the function of the protein produced by that gene, but the technology has limits. For example, if the deleted gene was responsible for producing a protein critical to growth, the knockout mouse won't survive long enough to be studied properly.

The third method for discovering gene function provides an alternative to the dead-mouse dilemma: Using antisense, it's possible to "turn off" the gene in a cell culture or an animal model and then observe the results. Not only is this a better method for isolating genes critical to development, it's also faster than using knockout mice. Many companies use this method to determine gene function, and Isis

Pharmaceuticals, which has some strong patents in antisense, is turning it into a separate business. In one special condition, antisense has an appealing advantage over gene comparison and knockout mice: If it turns out that the protein produced by the gene is causing disease, the information used in detecting its function via antisense (that is, by turning off the gene's production of the protein) can then be used directly to prepare an antisense drug to combat the disease.

To bolster its understanding of human gene functions, functional genomics also looks to identify similar genes in other organisms, which can then be altered and studied to reveal more about their particular roles. Through gene modification experiments in other organisms, biotech has already learned a lot about disease processes. This has led to better models of diseases, which inform drug development, thereby increasing the chances for the resulting drugs to be effective when they get into human clinical trials. Functional genomics should continue to increase the breadth and depth of this process going forward.

ICOS provides a great example of how the genetic similarity through evolution can be an asset in drug development. In the process of drug screening (determining drug effectiveness), some of ICOS's founding scientists discovered a novel use for, of all organisms, yeast. Yeast has a type of phosphodiesterase enzyme (PDE) that is essential to its ability to divide and survive. Humans have a family of at least seven different types of PDEs, which deactivate messengers inside a cell and perform other critical functions in a number of different cell types. While a number of approved drugs work by inhibiting some of these PDEs, potential drugs to inhibit other classes of PDEs have run into issues with side effects.

Upon spotting the PDE parallel between yeast and humans, the ICOS scientists took advantage of it by cloning the gene for each type of human PDE into yeast, replacing the yeast's normal gene. Then they tested small molecule drugs to determine which ones were selective inhibitors of a specific PDE—a drug that inhibited a specific PDE would prevent the growth of only the yeast strain that had been genetically engineered with that specific PDE. Thanks to this process, ICOS is now in late-stage testing of its molecule for treating male erectile dysfunction by inhibiting a class-five PDE. This drug appears to have a number of advantages over Pfizer's market-leading Viagra, including fewer side effects. ICOS is also developing an inhibitor of a class-four PDE that appears to be promising in the treatment of inflammation.

How Products Will Result from Genomics

When people talk about the length of time it takes to get a drug to market, they're usually referring to the development of an orally available small molecule drug. Again, these drugs are the bastions of the large drug companies (historically accounting for most of their sales), and they are the source for most of the studies on how long it takes and how much it costs to successfully bring a drug to market. Based on observations of traditional small molecule drugs, the benchmarks are eight to ten years for development and $500 million to successfully produce a new product. The cost figure factors in the expense of subsidizing other products that have failed in trials.

In the new age of biotech, companies can circumvent these dyed-in-the-wool standards for drug development. For one thing, it's possible (though still quite rare) for a properly focused biotech company to develop a new drug for as little as $50 million. And in developing drugs from genomics information, there are possibilities beyond small molecule drugs, creating further opportunities for breaking conventional rules for lead time and expense.

Since genes directly produce proteins, genetic information can be used to produce a protein that would be useful as a drug. People sometimes talk about genomics as though it were a new sector, but in its basic methodology of mapping proteins to genes, it's practically old-fashioned—most of the early drugs produced by the biotech industry came from identifying genes that coded for useful proteins, then using recombinant DNA technology to produce large quantities of these proteins. Amgen's Epogen and Neupogen and Genentech's Activase and human growth hormone (HGH) are all made from naturally occurring human proteins. Beyond these well-known drugs, a number of proteins identified in the sequencing of the human genome are now in clinical trials.

Genetic information can also be used directly as a therapy for some illnesses. When a disease is caused by the lack of a specific protein, the insertion of the relevant genes into cells can instruct the body to make the protein internally. Although the concept of gene therapy is simple, it has turned out to be very difficult to make it work in humans. Periodic bouts of negative publicity, coupled with the length of time it has taken to produce results, have made most observers pessimistic about gene therapy's prospects. But there has been progress. Recent gains in understanding on how to get genes inside the desired cells will make it relatively easy to use the same techniques to deliver other genes. In addition, late-stage clinical trials are now under way using gene therapy to treat cancer, and the first products are likely to be on the market in a couple of years. Gene therapies to treat genetic diseases such as cystic fibrosis are further away from market, but researchers are rapidly resolving the problems. Once gene therapy is commercialized, the development track for subsequent products will be much easier.

When a disease is caused by overproduction of a specific protein, genetic information provides a quick way to stop that production. Genetic information is transformed into proteins by the production of messenger RNA, a step that provides a target for intervention. RNA can be destroyed or disabled using either antisense or ribozymes, which are naturally occuring pieces of RNA that can be directed to selectively inhibit any faulty messenger RNA. These techniques have also been hard to commercialize, but as progress continues, there should be a number of drugs on the market using antisense and ribozymes, with Isis and Ribozyme Pharmaceuticals being the companies to watch. One of the interesting advantages of this technology is that it can also be used to prevent bacteria and viruses from replicating by stopping their procuction of proteins.

Some recently discovered genes code for receptors on the surface of cells, as mentioned in the discussion of cancer in the previous chapter. In these cases, the genes can be "turned off" by the use of monoclonal antibodies that attach to the receptor and prevent it from receiving its signal. This is also a technique that can be used more quickly now that it has been successfully commercialized. Genentech's Herceptin and ImClone Systems' Erbitux treat cancer with this method.

While the oral small molecule drugs will always be the chief focus of the major drug companies, the first marketable products from the Human Genome Project are likely to come from these new methods. The net effect of the new approaches to creating drugs could be dramatic in the near future; genomics may play a role in cutting the eight- to ten-year timetable for drug development in half, an exciting possibility for cutting drug costs, expanding markets, and (eventually) delivering value to investors.

Investing in Genomics

There has always been and will continue to be a lot of hype surrounding genomics, with an emphasis on the scientific break-throughs and how important each specific piece of technology will be. In evaluating genomics companies as potential investments, however, the key questions are traditional and hype-free: How and when are they going to make money, and what does the competitive terrain look like?

Most of the genomics companies started as tools companies, with the concept of selling information or services to other companies to assist in their drug development process. The original financing for Human Genome Sciences (HGS), for example, came from a large corporate contract with SmithKline Beecham (SKB), which is now part of Glaxo SmithKline. HGS and The Institute for Genomic Research (TIGR), its nonprofit affiliate, were slated to do the sequencing and provide the genetic information to SKB, which would then identify targets for the development of small molecule drugs. Within a few years, when HGS and SKB discovered that the number of potential targets exceeded SKB's scope, they began to sign deals to sell this information to other large drug companies, generating cash flows that have since subsidized much of HGS's research. HGS retained the rights to use the genetic information in the development of protein drugs as well as in gene therapy and antisense. HGS now has five human proteins in clinical development as drugs, and should increasingly be viewed as a drug development company.

Some investors still believe that HGS will end up with a lot of valuable patents because of its early work in wholesale gene sequencing. This seems unlikely to me, particularly since the patent office has continued to tighten its delineation of what makes gene information patentable. I had these doubts from the beginning, so it's gratifying to hear a growing consensus question the worth of these potential patents. Even Craig Venter, who as president of TIGR and lead scientist on HGS's sequencing efforts voiced his pride over their work and its value as intellectual property, has reversed his position. Venter, until recently CEO of Celera, now says publicly that HGS's many patent applications based on his former work hold little value. Now I agree with him.

Like HGS, most of the original genomics tools companies focused on gene sequencing. More recently, the emphasis seems to have shifted to functional genomics companies, as investors recognize that with the human genome sequenced, the thrust is now figuring out what the proteins produced by these genes actually do. This shift will position some of these proteins to become prime targets for new drug development.

Functional genomics is a critical area, but it is hard to know which companies have the most valuable technology and how much money they will be able to make selling their skills and technology. Most of the deals functional genomics companies are making include royalties from any products their partners develop based on the information they provide. The problem for investors is that these royalties are likely to be many years away. Investors may become impatient when, in a few years, basic business slows down and all they can do is wait for uncertain royalties on years-away earnings from drugs still in early development.

The one gene sequencing company that has continued to be a tools company is Incyte Genomics. It started with the model of selling information to a large number of customers and has done deals with most of the large drug companies. After turning profitable in 1997, Incyte recognized that with sequencing nearing an end, the priority would turn to making sense of the sequencing information. As a result, it made a large investment in increasing its bioinformatics capability. This put the company in the red in 1999, and Wall Street analysts turned negative. I believe, however, that this was a wise decision, and I expect Incyte to be a survivor as a result. To me, the only questions surrounding Incyte have to do with valuation. How long will it be able to continue to grow? What's the value of the many patents it has been issued (with many more pending)? I'm not the only one searching for answers to these difficult questions, as is illustrated by Incyte's price volatility over the last couple of years. Adjusted for a September 2000 split, the stock sold as high as $144 on February 25, 2000, and as low as $11 in the first half of 2001. Even though it has more than $500 million in cash, roughly $200 million in annual revenues, and plans to develop its own drugs, Incyte currently trades at $15, giving it a market cap of just under $1 billion, and making Incyte an attractive vehicle for participating in genomics.

The excitement about the genomics sector has greatly increased the number of bioinformatics companies. A number of them have come public, but due to bioinformatics' more modest capital requirements, there are many more private companies. Most of these companies will develop and sell software, a business model that has been well-tested in the high-tech world. It remains to be seen, though, how large this market is for biotech and how much money these companies can make. We get some information from an example of one of the successful exit strategies for companies in this area—sale to a larger tools company. Pharmacopeia, one of the early companies selling combinatorial chemistry as a tool, acquired Molecular Simulations. Along with some smaller software acquisitions, Molecular Simulations' growth has been an important contributor to Pharmacopeia's results, accounting for about two-thirds of 2000 revenues of $119 million.

Evaluating genomics companies that are exclusively tools companies is easier—they have significant revenues, and most of them are profitable. Investors can use conventional valuation models such as PE ratios or a multiple of revenues. The one snag comes when these companies get royalties from the products they have helped their clients develop, as many of them do. Besides the problem with impatience mentioned above, the fact that royalty rates usually are not disclosed adds further difficulty to the task of estimating how long it will take these products to get to market and how much revenue they will generate.

Increasingly, the valuation of the genomics companies shifting into product companies should be based on three factors: The products they're developing, when the products will be on the market, and how large a market the products will serve. Investors need to recognize when valuations don't match these criteria. For example, HGS now has a larger market capitalization than most of its competitors because it has products in clinical trials. Yet when compared with other companies that have been developing products for a longer period, the potential for HGS's products appears to justify only a small part of the current market capitalization.

At present, these types of microdevelopments are the norm in genomics. Companies are full of prospects, but often (understandably, at this stage) short on specifics, making genomics a tough area for investors. Certainly price matters (as it does in any investing decision), and at present there are a handful of high-profile companies (most notably Incyte, Millennium, and Celera) that are currently trading at roughly 20 percent of their all-time highs, thereby meriting a look on valuation alone. Millennium is doing an intelligent job of using acquisitions to move ahead as a product company, with the recent acquisition of Cor Therapeutics adding both an attractive marketed product (Integrilin) and expertise on cardiovascular disease. Meanwhile, Celera's acquisition of Axys Therepeutics has greatly increased its drug development capability. But for the most part, it's time to watch and wait in the genomics sector. The long run looks promising—the impressive accomplishments in the field may create new possibilities for drug developers. But the story is still in its early moments, and no one can map out genomics' future.

How to Invest in Biotech Stocks

Thus far, we have toured biotechnology's terrain, history, and cutting edge. We've also looked at my own motivation and philosophy for investing in the sector—why I believe this is biotech's moment in the sun, and what general principles I use to guide my investment decisions. Now it's time to move from theory to practice, to work through the mechanics of biotech investing—how to research companies, identify stocks worth investing in, and gauge when to buy and sell. This chapter moves through the basic mechanics, leaving a handful of more advanced investing issues (how to evaluate a biotech company's drug development process, for example) that require deeper explorations for later chapters. In the meantime, by applying the basics described in this chapter against the backdrop of all that we've already covered, you should be able to start picking stocks.

Screening Biotech Stocks

For a long-term value investor in this sector, the ideal stock belongs to a company with biotech's version of solid fundamentals—excellent science, good management, and a solid financial position. Before we examine each of these in further detail, it's important to reiterate one of the realities of the sector: At present, the vast majority of biotech companies are not profitable. In some of biotech's strongest companies (and best investing opportunities), traditional measures for determining investor value often don't apply. Excellent science and good management don't always translate to already-approved, market-tested products. And solid financial position doesn't automatically imply earnings. Fortunately, there are proxies for earnings, methods for separating fact from fiction in company news, and ways to evaluate corporate strategies that don't require traditional financial measures.

Evaluating Science

Generally speaking, the founders of biotech companies are scientists. They start companies with discoveries they've made or technologies they've created, and they hire other scientists and managers who share their vision. While they may or may not be motivated by money, it's a safe bet that the founding scientists are true believers in their innovations, enthusiastic to the point of being biased, a point of view that's often reflected throughout their companies.

The bias created from this enthusiasm is what makes assessing a biotech's key technologies difficult. If you narrow your focus to what the company's reporting about itself, not only will you fall into the obvious trap of failing to consider the source, but you'll also find yourself in a more subtle tangle: You'll overemphasize the science. This is a critical mistake in biotech investing; the quality of the science is undeniably important, but unless you frame it in terms of markets, you'll quickly become lost. The way out is to ask yourself early and often how a company's science translates (or will translate) to earnings.

When I'm trying to gauge the quality of a science within a specific company, I like to talk to the competition. Naturally, they tend to be biased when analyzing competitors, but their biases are usually in the opposite direction of the company I'm researching. Although I have to take everything I hear from these sources with a grain of salt, hearing the acknowledgments and criticisms of the opposite side is a great way to quickly identify key scientific issues.

If you take into account the fact that there are different kinds of companies in biotech, each with different competitive concerns, and you look at what their competitors are saying, you'll be able to learn what the right questions are to ask about the quality of science in the company you're examining.

If I'm interested in a biotech drug company, I know that if it can successfully bring a drug to market, it has a good chance of enjoying high profit margins as a result of strong patent protection. I also know that biotech drugs require prodigious investments of time and money to bring products to market (ten years and $500 million per drug aren't unheard of). And I know that its competitors are pursuing the same goal—combatting a particular disease or condition—though probably through markedly different scientific approaches. As a result, competitor insights on the company in question will point out where I might need to focus. Are they questioning the likelihood of the company's product making it through the various stages of clinical testing? Are they championing the many or few alternatives to the company's scientific approach to the problem? Are they scaling back or redoubling their own efforts to find alternative solutions? How do they assess the size of the potential markets their competing products are trying to reach?

If I'm interested in a diagnostics or tools company, I know that it is capable of bringing products to market faster than biotech drug companies. But I also know that its patents tend to be far weaker, and that diagnostics and tools are extremely competitive subsegments of the industry. Diagnostics companies are susceptible to "knockoff" products from competitors, and tools companies face the threat of the biotech companies they serve developing their own tools in-house, eliminating the need for their services. Questions worth asking include: Are competitors more worried about who has the superior product or about who can market it better? Are they working to catch up to the technologies of the company I'm interested in, or do they believe they're in the lead? Looking at the market as a whole, are they more concerned with marketing or science issues?

Of course, which issues emerge as the most important depend on the company (and competitors) in question. And you'll have to do some digging just to find out who a company's competitors are (we'll run through a list of research resources later in the chapter). But once you identify the competition and learn what it's saying about the company that has attracted your interest, you'll be able to pick up on patterns, sort through the real issues, and track the evidence as it develops. You won't master every nuance of the science, but you don't need to—instead, you'll find that by keeping the focus on how the science translates to markets, you'll be able to learn what you need to know to make investment decisions.

In addition to turning to competitors in building your own valuation model for the quality of a company's science, biotech boasts a pair of role models for scientific excellence: Chiron and Genentech. Both companies have managed to keep their research efforts energized and focused, while never losing sight of the market demands. Any company whose approach to science compares favorably with theirs merits further attention.

From the very beginning, the three founders of Chiron, all Ph.D.s, drew on their reputations and contacts to attract other excellent scientists to the company. Building a deep bench of scientific talent has been critical to Chiron's success. Though a number of its early products failed in clinical trials, a single major scientific breakthrough kept the company moving ahead—the discovery of the hepatitis C virus (HCV). Chiron's discovery of HCV subsequently enabled it to develop diagnostic tests to screen blood and prevent HCV from being transmitted by blood transfusions. Prior to Chiron's discovery, both hepatitis A and hepatitis B were well-known and treatable by vaccination, but scientists recognized the existence of at least one other unidentified virus, hepatitis non-A non-B. During this period, a number of efforts had been made to identify this virus, but all of them had failed.

I remember discussing Chiron's hepatitis non-A non-B research with its CEO, Ed Penhoet, right around the time the company discovered HCV. He explained why the research was important, some of the scientific challenges involved, and the large business opportunity it presented. I asked him about competition, including work being done in universities. He explained that the amount of money and time required made it highly unlikely that any university would achieve a breakthrough; they simply weren't capable of coming up with the multimillions needed to fund the work. Chiron had the money, the talent, and (as I learned from my conversations) a CEO who understood both the science and the market potential of the research. In May 1988, Chiron announced the discovery of HCV, and less than two years later it had its first blood screening test on the market. That business line now generates somewhere in the neighborhood of $80 million in pretax profits for Chiron annually.

And the company has continued to build on the business: In 2002, the company began selling new HCV diagnostics, which test for the virus directly rather than tagging the antibodies produced by the body after infection. This earlier detection reduces the number of blood donations that can transmit the virus to the recipient. Chiron is commercializing these diagnostics, called nucleic acid tests, in a joint venture with Genprobe (a subsidiary of the Japanese drug company Chugai), an arrangement that will add another major source of profits for Chiron from this initial discovery of HCV. Still to come will be royalties from the companies who have licensed Chiron's patents to develop drugs to treat HCV.

Like Chiron, Genentech has built its reputation on excellent science, beginning with its cofounders. Bob Swanson was a venture capitalist, but his enthusiasm for what Genentech could accomplish was key to attracting the many talented scientists to the company. Herb Boyer was the codiscoverer of one of biotech's enabling technologies, recombinant DNA. Boyer was behind one of Genentech's secrets to success: He decided to encourage Genentech's scientists to publish in peer-reviewed scientific journals. This pro-publishing approach contrasted sharply with the large drug companies, who feared that peer-reviewed publications helped the competition. Talented scientists flocked to Genentech as a result of the difference, drawn to a company that seemed to position itself as a vehicle for changing medicine's future, with profits as a secondary motive to science.

Interestingly, the scientific reputation of Genentech slipped between 1990 and 1995, the years in which Kirk Raab led the company as its CEO. Raab, whose background was in sales, emphasized marketing initiatives, an approach that caused a number of top scientists to leave the company. In 1995, Genentech replaced Raab with Art Levinson, a scientist, and subsequently has seen its science reputation rebound, as the company has done an excellent job of moving more products into human clinical trials.

In recent years, there have been a number of companies founded by managers from Genentech and Chiron, and managers from these two companies have also been recruited to run smaller biotech companies as CEOs. This knowledge/experience transfer from biotech's scientific flagships will benefit the entire industry in the coming years, and the companies run by Chiron and Genentech alumni are well worth watching.

Assessing Management

At least in one respect, biotechnology is no different than any other industry: Good management matters. Within the sector, the distinguishing characteristics of good management include the ability to recruit scientific talent, skill in managing creative (and perhaps idiosyncratic) employees, a firm grasp of how to shepherd products all the way through to FDA approval and patent issuance, and an acumen for raising money. Complicating matters further is the fact that the subjective skills of good biotech management are interdependent. For example, having money in the bank allows managers to conduct more clinical trials, thereby increasing the chances for the success of individual products (or reducing the company's overall risk by putting multiple products into testing). So in a sense, the quality of management in science is a function of fund-raising ability.

Ideally, the best way to judge these interdependent, subjective strengths is through objective results—a difficult proposition in an industry where so many companies lack revenues or even market-ready products. Wall Street analysts frequently stumble when they run up against this problem; they'll describe a company as well-managed based on recent price action in the stock, even though a closer inspection of management practices might reveal causes for concern. Feeding into this problem of misperception is a "free ride" effect: In the short term, an approved product enjoying steady sales growth can cover for a multitude of managerial sins. Even if management is doing a poor job on activities with long-run implications—steadily developing new products, for example—an already approved drug thriving in the market can keep company perceptions strong and the stock price high in the short run.

Amgen provides a good illustration of this effect. Following the approval of its second product, Neupogen, in 1991, Amgen failed to put anything else on the market for the next six years. Even though it committed to the largest research and development expenditures in the industry, Amgen only managed to break its six-year dry spell with an approval for a product that took twelve years to move through clinical trials and ultimately generated weak sales totals. Despite this lackluster performance, the markets didn't punish Amgen's management. The markets didn't react even when Amgen failed to take advantage of its high stock price and considerable financial resources to acquire biotech business lines or companies. For all its financial power, Amgen made but one purchase, of Synergen in 1994, paying only a small premium over assets for it. Why did Wall Street ignore the obvious signs of subpar management? Because of the power of Epogen's and Neupogen's steady growth in sales and profits. These products marketed with great skill carried Amgen through the long rough patch, until management regained its footing with a number of recent product approvals.

While several companies have covered for brief spells of management error with the success of an already approved product, it's dangerous to conclude that short-term management isn't important. In many respects, Amgen was unusually fortunate; the vast majority of companies lack the resources to ride out such long dry spells. Nonetheless, if a biotech can temporarily hide mistakes, and/or it doesn't yet have any products on the market, how can an investor evaluate the quality of the company's management?

Certainly, there's no substitute for doing basic research—learning who a company's officers are and what their vision for the company is, the straightforward stuff of annual reports and articles. But in addition to this, I recommend looking for three elements that I believe are hints that a company has good management in place.

First, it helps to remember that in biotech, as in any other industry, companies of different sizes and stages of maturity require different managerial approaches. More than anything else, a new biotech company seeking to develop and commercialize some exciting new technology needs scientific leadership and fund-raising firepower. A company with products in later stages of development needs management that can design and guide clinical trials, as well as negotiate corporate partnerships. In mature biotech companies with approved products, marketing skills come to the fore. The obvious implication is to make sure the backgrounds of the management match the stage of development that the company is in. Where there's a mismatch, there's an opening for trouble.

~ Second, it's important to make sure that the company you're researching has a steady process of product development. Is the research department well-funded? What processes is it examining at present? How many products are being tested? Are there products in some or all of the various stages of testing? No biotech can guarantee product approvals, but the more the product development process has the feel of an assembly line, the better the chances that the company has strong management.

And third, generally speaking, the more scientists a biotech has at or near the top of its management, the better. Of course this is a bit of an oversimplification, but it's one I believe has some merit. The reason I look for scientists at the top has to do with the overall quality of workforce it takes for a biotech to succeed. Talented biotech scientists are always in short supply. They're also often challenging to manage, as many come out of academic environments and need to adjust to corporate structures. It's no accident that the companies that have been the most successful in recruiting and retaining these individuals have also earned reputations for excelling in science, a key to biotech success. I also believe it's no accident that the key to this recruiting success has been having scientists in top management, people who know what to look for in building their workforces. Scientists at the top create an environment to encourage good science throughout the company.

Understanding the Financial Position

In biotech, money in the bank reduces risk. Well-funded companies have the competitive advantage of superior product pipelines—they can research more broadly and deeply, conduct more clinical tests, and pursue a number of products simultaneously. They can also endure the failure of individual products and ride out dry spells in the capital markets, when raising money is difficult. And they can negotiate partnerships with other companies from a position of strength. Having sufficient funding doesn't ensure success in biotech, but lacking it restricts options and reduces prospects.

In an industry where the majority of product development attempts fail, the safest approach to investing is to look for companies with cash sufficient to fund one to two years' worth of operating expenses. There are times, however, when market conditions render this approach completely impractical, leaving potential investors with the next-best alternative: assessing a company's ability to raise funds in the future. This is a subjective process; it's hard to gauge a management team's zeal and intelligence, which seem to be key to raising money. Looking for objective measures, I find that companies whose fund-raising executives have large pharmaceutical company experience on their résumés appear to have an advantage. In fact, the capacity to raise funds is the only area these executives intrinsically have a leg up on the competition—possessing large pharmaceutical company credentials seems to bring contacts that ease negotiations for corporate partnerships and open doors for financing.

Beyond looking at large pharmaceutical company experience among the executives, perhaps the only other measure of fund-raising ability worth considering is the quality of the company's product development. Clearly, successful product development can lead to increased valuations, which opens the door to financing opportunities. And even if the company fails in its own fund-raising efforts, if its technology is successful the company becomes an attractive acquisition target.

In favorable financing conditions, some savvier start-ups have found success by raising additional capital while still working on their initial technology—then, even after their first approaches failed, they had the resources to move on to other things. Gilead, for example, raised a lot of money while focusing on antisense products; when the company couldn't make them work, it had the means to develop other products. Throughout the company's early failures, Wall Street remained positive in its assessments of Gilead, in no small part because of the persistence and success of the company's fund-raising efforts. Not only did Gilead's ample cash reserves reduce risk, but also the fees Wall Street earned from the fund-raising ensured sponsorship by the investment banks, keeping the company in the eye of the capital markets. Unfortunately, in biotech, the Gileads are the exception to the rule. When it comes to solid financial position, you're better off looking for cash on hand first, successful technology second, and executive ties to large pharmaceutical companies third.

Where to Find Information
for Screening Biotech Companies

Today, an individual investor with an Internet account has easy, free access to all the information needed to screen biotech companies. With the standard reports offered by a handful of financial, corporate, and medical web sites, the individual investor can go a long way toward understanding the financial position as well as the quality of management and science of a given company. A good starting point is Yahoo! Finance (http:\\finance.yahoo.com, or type in www.yahoo.com, then click on the Finance/Quotes section). You can look up companies by name or ticker symbol and find a brief description of what the companies do, the names of their senior officers, links to articles about the stocks, and basic financial information, including earnings and operating ratios. Using Yahoo! Finance, you can also pull up charts of stock price performance by day, week, month, and year, going back at least five years (sometimes further, depending on the company). If you're interested in even better charting, Big Charts (www.bigcharts.com) merits a look. It's a good place to pull up company charts, as well as charts for indexes such as the BTK.

For more detailed information on operations, I recommend looking at the web sites of the companies attracting your interest. In addition to providing access to annual report information (including balance sheets and income statements), the corporate sites tend to do a good job of explaining the science of the company—what the drugs do, what the potential markets are, where the drugs are in the development process.

For access to the financial documents Wall Street analysts use to assess what companies are doing, you can view a company's SEC filings (including 10Ks and 10Qs—changes in security status and quarterly earnings reports) at 10K Wizard (www.10kwizard.com). You can search this site using company names or ticker symbols and view all the recent SEC activity. The best source for historical information on mergers and corporate partnerships is Recombinant Capital (www.Recap.com).

As you build your own opinions about the potential for a company, it's worth taking a look at what Wall Street has to say. Despite my skepticism about the recommendations of sell-side analysts, their reports can be good sources of detailed company information. Interestingly, the most valuable details are often found in reports written by analysts who work for one of the company's underwriters. These analysts are sometimes privy to corporate information that's not widely disseminated, such as royalty rates on products or a company's internal estimates and expectations for clinical trials. They can also be good sources for uncovering a company's short- and long-term strategies. Corporate web sites are a good place to find out who a biotech company's underwriters are. From there, you can look up the underwriters' web sites and find their analyst reports. When read with a grain of salt (with more attention paid to the facts than the recommendations), these reports are valuable.

If you have an interest in delving deeper into the science, the National Institutes of Health has a comprehensive site for tracking clinical trials (www.clinicaltrials.gov). The magazines *Science* and *Scientific American* are also good sources for keeping up with what's happening in biotech research, although both periodicals are sometimes difficult for the layperson to read. Finally, in an industry laden with multisyllabic names for conditions, diseases, procedures, and drugs, reference books can be quite valuable in turning technospeak into English. *The American Medical Association Encyclopedia of Medicine* is fairly reader-friendly, and *Stedman's Medical Dictionary* is the standard for medical language. For a catalog of drugs, the *Physicians' Desk Reference*, or PDR, is the definitive source.

Valuation Rules of Thumb

After you've screened a company by assessing its science, management, and current financial position, it's time to determine whether its stock is worth buying. This is a sticking point for many value investors, who balk at putting money in biotech companies because they can't figure out how to arrive at a fair price for the stocks. The problem is particularly acute among companies that aren't yet profitable.

The most important drivers of value in a biotech company are self-evident: the earnings potential of products both on the market and in development and the intellectual property and skills of the employees and scientific advisers. Because it's hard to peg tangible dollar figures to each of these drivers, biotech stock prices are often volatile. When the markets focus on the immense potential for the sector and stock prices are climbing, it's easy to justify high prices. However, when the sector falls out of favor and prices are in decline, it's just as easy to believe that the stocks have further to fall. You'll fare better investing in biotech companies if you have some way to feel comfortable with the underlying values. Fortunately, there are a few rules of thumb that can help.

Valuing Profitable Biotech Companies: Translating Growth Rates into Stock Prices

In terms of valuation, a profitable biotech company can be viewed as an exceptional drug company. Typically, its growth rate and research and development expense ratio exceed those of an average pharmaceutical company, thereby justifying greater-than-average valuations. As an avowed growth stock investor, I've run across a number of complex mathematical models for valuing profitable growth stocks such as the profitable biotech, but in their place, I have found that a simple rule of thumb suffices: If a company's price-to-earnings (PE) ratio is double its growth rate, then the stock is fairly priced. For example, an industrial company whose earnings grow at an annual rate of 5 percent deserves a multiple of 10, and a pharmaceutical company whose earnings grow 12 percent annually merits a 24 PE.

The growth rates of most profitable biotech companies range between 20 percent and 25 percent, justifying PEs between 40 and 50. The growth rate for profitable biotech companies is historically higher than the large pharmaceutical company average, an edge that's likely to continue, because in terms of revenue percentages profitable biotech companies outspend large pharmaceutical companies in research and development. The typical pharmaceutical company spends between 12 and 15 percent of its revenues on R&D, whereas most biotech companies with significant product revenues spend around 25 percent. When you look at a profitable biotech company, always note the rate of R&D spending; if it's more than 25 percent and you believe in the company's technology and management, an even higher multiple of current earnings can be justified.

By taking the growth rates of profitable biotech companies and translating them into PE ratios, you set up a powerful platform for comparing stocks. As in any other industry sector, viewing stocks in terms of PEs enables the investor to make apples-to-apples comparisons among companies of different sizes with different volumes of shares outstanding. Wide disparities in PEs, for example, between two biotech companies can prompt the right questions: Does one company have earnings that are artificially depressed? Or does the other company have earnings that are likely to grow much faster? You can take advantage of PEs to identify mismatches between comparable biotech companies, or to spot valuation lags across the entire sector (that is, industry growth rates should justify higher PEs). Among profitable biotech stocks, these are where the investing opportunities are found.

Using Market Caps to Compare As-Yet-Unprofitable Biotech Companies

Using growth rates to construct PE ratios is a simple, versatile method for comparing stocks, but most biotech companies aren't profitable, and therefore don't have PE ratios. One solution is to avoid biotech companies that aren't yet producing earnings, but this strategy reduces investment opportunities too drastically, eliminating some of the most promising companies within the sector.

Investment professionals don't avoid unprofitable companies, but they do try to analyze them in the same terms as profitable ones. When faced with assessing a promising but as-yet-unprofitable biotech, Wall Street analysts do their best to value the company based on future earnings. To estimate future earnings, analysts have to guess when products will be approved and then guess the revenue growth rates year after year for each product. They then discount these projected future earnings streams using a fairly arbitrary rate of return and divide the total by the number of shares outstanding, thus arriving at an estimated earnings per share.

Depending on your outlook, this process is brave, optimistic, misguided, or futile. I'll reserve my own judgment, except to say that the process is full of vexing assumptions. The discount rate varies from analyst to analyst, and the sizes and rates of growth of income streams are pure projections. As a result of these built-in assumptions and guesstimates, analysts arrive at earnings numbers I often find hard to accept. They insist on projecting each quarter to the nearest penny, offering up oddly precise earnings estimates in a financially imprecise sector. Personally, I would assign much greater credibility to analysts who dropped the penny-perfect estimates in favor of broader ranges ($1.50 to $2.00 a share, for example, rather than $1.61 per share), and then discussed the important variables that helped determine the ranges.

If you choose not to rely on analyst estimates, what other approach can you take to value unprofitable companies? I prefer to use total market capitalization as a proxy for the PE ratio. It's easy to calculate—simply multiply the current stock price by the number of shares outstanding. Once you have a company's market cap, you can match it against your expectations for the company's future revenues from its products. As a benchmark figure, the market caps for most profitable biotech companies run right around ten times the revenues. I'm often amazed by how this simple calculation and comparison technique alerts me to the disparities between stocks I'm considering. One stock might have an enormous market cap, far out of proportion to the earnings potential of the products the underlying company has in development, whereas another stock might have a small cap relative to its cash position and the earning potential of its emerging products—a combination of factors that signals an investment opportunity.

The market capitalizations of biotech companies vary tremendously. The current leader is Amgen, whose total market cap exceeds $70 billion. At the other extreme, we find a number of companies with interesting compounds advancing through clinical trials, money in the bank, and exciting technology with market caps in the $200 million to $500 million range. For companies with such modest market caps, the impact of one successful drug can be dramatic.

Sometimes it's instructive to compare currently popular biotech companies with less-glamorous biotech companies on the basis of market capitalizations alone. This approach is a particularly effective method to avoid getting swept up in the fever of a hot segment within the industry; by comparing the market caps of a hot company and an unrelated biotech—even one that has no products that directly compete with those of the favored company—you can often spot market overvaluations. In fact, it's not unusual for the company that's out of the spotlight to emerge as the relative bargain in the comparison. For example, consider Human Genome Sciences, a genomics company with five products in clinical trials. HGS, basking in the genomics spotlight, also boasts $1.2 billion of net cash; its ability to raise such a considerable amount of money has resulted in a lot of Wall Street sponsorship—that is, analysts play close (and frequently favorable) attention to every move the company makes. This is great for HGS, but compare it to a company like Isis Pharmaceutical, which has eleven products in clinical trials. Not only does Isis have more products in testing, but its products also appear to have larger potential markets than those of HGS. Isis's lead product is in a final-stage trial to treat non-small-cell lung cancer, which causes more deaths in the United States than any other cancer and has no adequate treatment currently on the market. Isis's lead drug contrasts sharply with HGS's lead product, which is for wound healing, an area of medical inquiry in which a number of other products have disappointed in clinical trials; in fact, the lone wound healing product currently on the market (Chiron's Regranex, marketed by Johnson & Johnson) has generated only modest sales. Despite obvious advantages in every area of science and product development, Isis at present has a market capitalization of only $1.1 billion at its recent price of $23 a share. This is dwarfed by HGS's market capitalization of $5 billion at $40 a share. Looking at the companies and their market caps alone, HGS appears overpriced, and the less-celebrated Isis looks like the bargain.

Of course, in normal conditions (that is, when the markets aren't inflating the values of every company within a hot segment), comparing competing biotech companies on the basis of market capitalization can be a good method for finding investment opportunities. ImClone Systems, for example, is likely to receive approval for its lead anticancer drug, Erbitux (which treats colorectal cancer) during 2002. Erbitux is a monoclonal antibody drug that's directed at the epidermal growth factor (EGF) receptor, which is associated with at least half of all solid tumors. It's interesting to look at ImClone in relation to IDEC Pharmaceuticals, which sells another monoclonal antibody drug,

Rituxan, which also treats cancer. Rituxan targets an antigen that appears on B-cell lymphomas. Each year, roughly 55,000 patients are diagnosed with B-cell lymphomas. In comparison, each year there are 1 million reported cases of solid tumors. So ImClone's Erbitux addresses a market of about 500,000, which is about ten times that of IDEC's. In addition, ImClone's recent partnership with Bristol-Myers Squibb gives it a very strong marketing partner, plus $1 billion in cash up front. With its stock currently trading in the $50 range, ImClone has a market cap of $5.4 billion, whereas IDEC's stock, currently trading around $70, has a market cap of $10.8 billion. Although ImClone's stock has recently moved up sharply, it is still attractive relative to IDEC, boasting a far larger market and half the market cap.

Comparisons can be informative, but with an extra step, you can use the market cap approach to evaluate a company in isolation. Even without another biotech to compare it to, the question of valuing any biotech remains the same: Is it worth more or less than its current market cap? As a long-term value investor, I follow the Wall Street analysts' lead and find my answers to this question by making my own estimates of future revenue streams. Unlike the Wall Street analysts, however, I base my estimates not on shifting discount rates, but rather on biotech industry norms for value. For example, over the years biotech companies have periodically sold stable lines of business (products already on the market with consistent but unspectacular earnings power) to other biotech companies and large pharmaceutical companies. The going rate for these transactions is roughly four times annual product revenues, a multiple that reflects the high profit margins of drug products. This multiple also sets the floor for any valuation I make for projected revenues. For a new product enjoying rapid sales growth, the sales multiple can rise as high as ten times annual revenues.

The next step requires some digging—you'll have to make revenue projections. Some of the approaches we've already discussed are useful here as well. For starters, this is one of the more valuable places to pit what the company in question projects against what its competitors are saying. The three major considerations to keep in mind (discussed in more depth in the chapters on disease and drug development) are as follows:

1. Market potential—What's the size of the overall market? What's a reasonable share the product might hope to capture? Is the number of competitors in the field stable or growing?

2. Time to market—How long will it be before the product is likely to be approved?

3. Development risk—Does the development risk for the product still lie ahead? Key determinants include results from clinical trials to date, the nature of the disease the drug addresses, and the type of product being developed.

Once you have your revenue projections for the one or more products a company has in development, you can assign a conservative or aggressive multiple to the company based on your assessment of its growth potential. Multiply the revenues by your multiple, and you have a projected market cap to compare against the actual market cap. If the projected figure far exceeds the actual figure, you may have an investment opportunity.

Let's look at an example. In mid-2001, ICOS filed for marketing approval for a new drug, Cialis, which will compete with Pfizer's Viagra to treat male erectile dysfunction. Clinical trials have shown that Cialis has both a quicker onset of action and a longer half-life than Viagra, and because it's more specific in its action, it appears to have fewer side effects. Pfizer anticipated 2001 worldwide revenues for Viagra to be in the neighborhood of $1.5 billion; given this figure, it's reasonable to estimate that Cialis could generate $1 billion in revenues within its second year on the market. Since ICOS is developing Cialis through a joint venture with Eli Lilly, we can credit ICOS with half of this $1 billion estimate. Given the promising growth prospects for the drug (as witnessed by Viagra's market performance to date), I assigned a fairly aggressive multiple of 8 to the projected revenue stream. In this model, which bases the valuation of the company entirely on the expected performance of Cialis, ICOS is worth $500 million multiplied by 8, or $4 billion. In some ways this is a conservative estimated market cap for ICOS, which has a deep product development pipeline, including two additional drugs in late-stage clinical trials. Nonetheless, in reality ICOS's market cap is below the Cialis-only valuation—trading at around $60 a share, ICOS checks in with a real-world valuation of only $3.6 billion. This indicates to me that the stock is still attractively priced, with substantial upside potential as other drugs in the pipeline move ahead.

A Few Words About Cash and Hard Assets

Cash and other hard assets aren't the most important drivers of valuation in biotech companies; for companies whose drugs are still in development, they're secondary elements to the main activity of trying to bring drugs to market. Nonetheless, they're easily assessed and merit consideration in the valuation process.

As I noted earlier, there's an industry rule of thumb regarding cash: If a company has enough funds to bankroll its operations, losses and all, for two years, it has sufficient cash reserves. There are many circumstances in which I'd consider investing in a company with lower levels of cash than this, but it increases the risk. Subpar reserves of funds can also cause other investors to balk at purchasing the stock, thereby keeping its price down. Fortunately, in the wake of the 1999–2000 biotech rally, most companies successfully raised money and are poised to fund their operations for well over two years on the proceeds, even if they fail to generate revenues.

After cash, the other main hard asset among biotech companies is manufacturing capacity. For companies that have products nearing approval, manufacturing facilities can be important. This is particularly true if the products are complex proteins or unique molecules that cannot be easily made by contract manufacturers. The importance of manufacturing was brought to investors' attention dramatically in 2000, when Immunex revealed that it couldn't keep up with demand for its lead product, Enbrel, because it had run out of manufacturing capacity and did not expect to bring new facilities online until June 2002. As in the case of cash reserves, it's best to consider manufacturing capacity as a check-off item after doing the research, calculations, and comparisons necessary to make company valuations.

When to Buy

Once you've screened a set of companies on their fundamentals and run your PE and/or market cap analyses, you may have identified a few bargain stocks. Before you invest, there's one more important question to address: Why are they bargains? Put more cynically, if you've been able to find these bargains, why hasn't everybody else? The secret to big returns in value investing lies in the answers to these questions. If you don't understand why companies are undervalued, you'll run the risk of buying in and watching, watching, watching as they go unnoticed by the market and stay undervalued. You're not looking for perpetual bargains, only temporary ones.

There are a number of reasons why temporary bargains come into being. Fear can create them—from time to time in biotech, the entire sector falls out of favor with the investment community, sometimes for irrational reasons. For example, in the early spring of 2001, biotech companies were thriving, but the devastating bear market in the technology stocks, led by the crash in Internet stocks, created a climate of fear in which investors bailed out of biotech companies as well. Guided by fear, investors didn't take into account the improving fundamentals and the ample cash of the typical biotech during that time—they just sold everything.

As stressful as such declines may be, they create bumper crops of bargain stocks; if the fundamentals of the underlying companies are strong, there's a good chance the valuations will eventually recover. Many of the best companies become available at attractive prices in the aftermath of slumps. And smaller cap stocks, usually the most heavily (and unfairly) punished during downturns, frequently offer the best values.

Broad downturns in the biotech markets not only breed bargains, but they also inherently contain the final element for value investing success: If the fundamentals are in place, the markets will eventually take notice of value they've ignored or mispriced, and stock prices will rise. It's the secret of value investing—you should only buy bargains when you've reason to believe the markets will eventually discover (or rediscover) the stocks.

Beyond periodic broad drops within the sector, you can look for other conditions to identify these kinds of temporary bargains. From

time to time, you'll find well-run biotech companies that aren't being supported by Wall Street (few analysts are recommending the
stock, or even following it). It's also a good sign when the stock has
little institutional ownership—in other words, the pension funds
and Fidelitys and insurance companies of the world have yet to buy
into the biotech gem you've uncovered. If insiders are snapping up
the stock but the rest of the world has yet to catch on, it's a good
sign of a potential bargain. There are even promising bargain conditions to be found among companies caught amid controversy—one
of the company's competitors may be bad-mouthing it or outdated
doubts about a company's technology persist, despite the fact that
the problems have already been resolved by the company. The key
is making the judgment that these temporary oversights or misper-
ceptions will eventually fall by the wayside, to be replaced by more
accurate valuations. In these situations, your research on fundamentals, earnings potential, and gaps between current and potential
market valuations puts you in the position to anticipate favorable
price movements.

In my own experience, I've usually come across a temporary bargain opportunity only after following a company for some time. In
other words, I look for good companies and then wait for them to
become bargains before buying in. For example, in late 1984, the
biotech stocks that had come public in 1983 were all declining in
price. The stocks of two of these companies, Amgen and Chiron,
had dropped enough to attract my attention. Since Chiron was close
by, I went over for a visit and came away convinced that it had good
management, excellent science, and a reasonable business plan. My
business partner and I then recommended Chiron's stock in the
MTSL in December 1984 at $4-5/8, a deep discount from its IPO
price of $12 from less than two years before. My interest in Amgen
developed during the spring of 1985 after talking with Bill Edwards,
one of Amgen's original venture capital investors. He assured me
that George Rathmann was an excellent manager for the company,
and on the strength of his recommendations and my own research,
we recommended Amgen in April 1985 at $5-3/8, substantially be-
low its IPO price of $18. Both companies have since brought excel-
lent results. At its recent $45, Chiron is up 39 times, while Amgen,
at a recent 56, is up over 550 times, both adjusted for splits.

The lesson: Even the biggest and best-known companies within the industry can temporarily turn into bargains. You may need to do some research, wait for long periods for the markets to come around, and endure tests of the courage of your convictions. But if you're patient, you'll have a chance at some terrific returns by putting your money in some of biotech's best (and least risky) companies.

Beyond the best-known companies, you can occasionally find some diamonds in the rough among smaller cap stocks. In 1986, a small investment firm in San Diego underwrote Agouron's IPO at a price of $10 per share. During a rather modest market correction in October 1990, Agouron tumbled to a low of $4, at which point we recommended its purchase in the MTSL. At $4, Agouron's total market cap was a mere $17 million, an irrationally low figure that emerged as a result of fear: A number of institutional buyers who'd invested in Agouron's secondary offering panicked and bailed out of the stock. These investors missed out on a tremendous ride by Agouron, which jumped to $90 after its first product approval in 1997 before eventually selling out to Warner Lambert in 1999 for $2.1 billion. Investors who got in on this temporary bargain in 1990, buying a stock no one wanted a part of, were rewarded with a more than thirtyfold return in nine years.

Agouron is an example of how bargains can emerge, persist, and then finally catch fire and become big winners. Remember that small cap stocks sometimes attract little or no attention from Wall Street analysts. In fact, many sell-side analysts restrict their coverage to the larger companies and the companies their firms have underwritten. In addition, institutional investors are wary of putting money into small caps because of liquidity issues. As a rule, they'd prefer to make a $1 million investment in a company with a market cap of $1 billion than in a comparable company with a market cap of $100 million, simply because the larger stock would be easier to trade in and out of if market conditions were to change.

On the other hand, if a company like Agouron starts to gain a little momentum in the market and its market cap grows, it can attract more attention—an ideal condition for a value investor who's bought in on a bargain. When a smaller biotech's stock price climbs, it's more likely to pick up analyst coverage when the market capitalization reaches a level that the analyst thinks will interest the institutions.

The market cap varies from institution to institution, but at present the two most critical price points are $500 million and $1 billion. When a stock like Agouron crosses each of these, Wall Street jumps in, and the momentum gains a life of its own.

A Final Word on Valuation

We've gone through a lot of techniques for identifying stocks in this chapter, maybe too many to absorb in one sitting. It's my hope, however, that as you look back on the material we've covered, you'll see that none of it is inherently difficult and that all of it is rooted in a measure of common sense. I also hope you'll see that by matching the techniques in this chapter to your own investing philosophy, you'll see the importance of developing and sticking to an overall approach to biotech investing. The combination of skills and approach will enable you to pick up bargains rather than panic at the bottom of a correction, as well as be patient if you believe in a company's fundamentals.

CHAPTER 8

Drug Development

Getting a drug on the market is the holy grail of the business of biotechnology. Few people, however, have any sense of how complex the process of developing drugs can be—even some of the people who run biotech companies have not always fully appreciated everything that is involved. Drug development demands an effective combination of science and business, executed over many years through several different stages.

By the time drugs become available to their intended patients, they have long, often convoluted histories. They have jumped through multiple proverbial "hoops," the last of which is the stringent approval process of the U.S. Food and Drug Administration (FDA). The FDA grants or denies approval of a drug based on data from three successive phases of clinical trials, conducted over many years on human subjects via cooperating medical clinics, as well as preclinical studies using laboratory animals. Of course, all of this stems from the discovery of a promising drug candidate, which often involves a new scientific breakthrough—the product of basic research.

Shepherding a drug through the entire process and gaining FDA marketing approval is an exceptional accomplishment. Most of the drugs that enter clinical trials—meaning that they showed enough potential in research and preclinical studies to warrant the major expense of a clinical trial—do not win approval. As a drug advances through the phases of clinical trials, though, its odds of success increase significantly, reaching 70 percent by the time it enters the final phase. Even in the final phase, however, it's difficult to interpret the odds. Some drugs that encounter problems here, like Genentech's Activase, which got a negative review from the FDA advisory panel, will gain approvals anyway. Others, like interleukin 2, which ran into toxicity issues in development by several companies, will be delayed for years as they prepare for resubmission before finally gaining approval.

Historically, biotech companies have achieved better overall approval percentages than large pharmaceutical companies—an edge primarily due to biotech's working more with protein drugs, which have less potential for toxicity than pharmaceuticals' usual work on small molecule drugs. The lower toxicity risk results in fewer failures in early clinical trials. Biotech companies also gain a greater number of new drug approvals each year than the pharmaceutical industry, a count that is growing annually.

While these rules of thumb give investors a useful starting point from which to consider drug development and approval, each potential drug has its own unique odds. Contributing factors include the type of drug, the disease it's designed to treat, and the degree to which the drug's target (in the body) has been validated, that is, confirmed as key in the disease activity. Companies with the best drug development will tailor each of their programs according to these factors, as well as take into account the drug's potential competition in its intended market.

Clearly, individual investors cannot expect to track each of the 300-plus biotech companies to keep tabs on the progress of the more than 200 products currently in late-stage clinical trials. But they can learn enough about the drug development process to ask the right questions, the answers to which will help them assess the risks involved in a specific drug development program. Underlying the obvious question of whether the drug will gain approval are other important questions on the key parameters of development time lines and convenience of use.

Answering these questions means applying some critical thought to weigh various possibilities. After all, the essential nature of clinical trials is that success is never certain. If we knew ahead of time that a drug would work and be safe, clinical trials would not be necessary. We can get a reasonable sense of the risk of a particular drug development program from considering relevant (if somewhat subjective) factors such as competitors' previous successes in a particular disease and the strength of earlier clinical trial results. In addition, the investor must consider the extent to which positive results are discounted by the current market price.

The last factor depends in part on how well the biotech company has sold Wall Street on its likely success. The more effectively the company has communicated its good news and potential (essentially "hyping" its own product), the greater the risk for the investor. More modest risk—along with potentially large rewards—comes from the company that has designed intelligent clinical trials but remains ignored by Wall Street. I like to find stocks before Wall Street knows about them for this very reason—the lower valuation reduces the risk and increases the potential profit. To this end, I give a lot of weight to the results from the conclusion of the second phase of the three phases of clinical trials, asking myself: Were the results only somewhat favorable, or were they very convincing? To my surprise, Wall Street does not always ask these key questions.

Sometimes investors will have to wait a while to get any information they can use to construct answers. As a potential drug undergoes study during a particular stage of clinical trials, there are no benchmarks for an investor to evaluate the trial's progress. To obtain the best statistics on a drug's efficacy, later-stage trials are usually "blinded," meaning that participating doctors and patients don't know which patients are taking the actual drug and which patients are taking the placebo. Only through the trial's completion, examination of results (merely favorable, or very compelling?), and advancement to the next stage (although the stages can overlap) can the investor know whether the drug shows promise.

Investors should beware of a possible pitfall here—the more they learn about the science of biotechnology and its development process, the more excited they get about its potential results. Becoming too attached to the science can be treacherous for a fundamental investor. Scientific breakthroughs that hold great long-term promise, such as genomics, don't necessarily translate to products and earnings.

That said, it's hard not to get excited about drug development. Drug development is the industry of biotechnology at work, taking the science and turning it into opportunity—for patients and for investors. We'll take a closer look, starting at the beginning.

Discovery

Drug discovery is the initial and most scientific part of the entire drug development process. Consisting of basic research on how to harness new scientific knowledge into a potential treatment application, drug discovery is the area where biotech companies have really distinguished themselves. In fact, many biotech companies founded in the past decade have formed in direct response to advances made by university scientists. These scientists' discoveries help explain the mysteries of the chemical, biological, and physical processes of the human body, but they rarely map to any immediate treatment or product. That's where a new or established biotech company comes in. Once any intellectual property issues have been resolved, a biotech company will take the findings from a major discovery and conduct basic research aimed at helping to commercialize the new knowledge. The key scientists often join the company or serve as its scientific advisers.

It is no coincidence that the largest concentrations of biotech companies have grown around major academic research institutions—the University of California's Berkeley and San Francisco campuses and Stanford in the San Francisco Bay Area, Harvard and MIT in Cambridge and Boston, and the University of California at San Diego, the Scripps Research Institute, and the Salk Institute in San Diego. Biotechnology depends on these research powerhouses to help propel its industry.

Often, the same scientific discovery will set more than one direction of research in motion. Take, for example, the discovery of the role that a particular protein, produced by a specific gene, plays in the progression of a disease. Researchers may work to develop an orally available small molecule drug to inhibit the action of this protein, or they could pursue an antisense drug to stop production of the protein altogether. Either of these routes could mean years of research, but the first will take much longer. Not only does the process of finding a small molecule that interacts in the desired way take years, but the resulting drug's synthetic nature increases the chance of it having an unexpected biological impact. This concern demands more stringent toxicity testing over longer periods of time.

In small molecule drug development, knowing the biological pathways of the disease and selecting the best target at which to address the disease are just the first steps. Next, researchers must establish a way to screen possible drug candidates, to see which ones "modify" or have an effect on the target. This is usually done in cell cultures, where researchers can see and measure any modifications that occur. Large pharmaceutical and biotech companies that have used this procedure for years have consequently developed vast libraries of chemicals to test as potential drugs. Although it's extremely unlikely that any of these chemicals will inadvertently match to yield the currently sought results, the chemicals that do interact with the target will provide leads indicating what characteristics an effective drug might need. Medicinal chemists can then modify the promising compounds and test their value.

The biotech industry has contributed significantly to the screening process by developing combinatorial chemistry. This science makes thousands or even millions of different chemical compounds, which can then be screened against promising drug targets. To assess all of these possibilities, drug developers must have a system that can rapidly screen a large number of compounds. Biotech companies have filled this need as well, developing new faster screening systems that they have licensed to large pharmaceutical companies.

Biotech companies have also found ways to determine which monoclonal antibodies might make good drug candidates for some diseases, as advances in genomics have made it easier for companies to identify the cell surface receptors that make attractive drug targets. With the progress that has been made lately in developing monoclonal antibodies, producing the drug candidates is reasonably quick.

Preclinical Studies

Of the product ideas explored in discovery, a few will show enough potential to warrant further research and testing. In the preclinical studies that follow, scientists examine promising compounds in animal models to see how they work in a more complex system. Preclinical studies help to determine a potential drug's efficacy and safety. Even though humans are the drug's final target, it takes a few years of investigation and analysis before the drug is refined enough to be tested in them.

The right animal model—one that reliably mimics the human disease—is critical in giving a good indication of a potential drug's worth. Specially bred and, more recently, genetically modified mice have become important new tools for demonstrating the biological interactions in a specific disease. Selective breeding of mice has established strains with disease symptoms (such as high cholesterol) that resemble those of human diseases. And "knockout" mice, with a single gene deleted, can be very helpful in testing drugs designed to remedy conditions where the lack of a protein (that the absent gene would have created) plays a significant role.

In addition to showing a drug's overall potential, results in animals will sometimes reveal minor problems as well, which suggest needed modifications to the initial compound. For example, the original compound may not be well absorbed when administered orally, so chemists will adapt it to solve that problem, without diminishing its overall effectiveness in interfering with the disease pathway. Medicinal chemists go through series of refinements for a potential drug, using proven techniques to make a compound easier to absorb or increase its water solubility without changing its medicinal qualities.

Another issue that comes up in this stage is how to increase the time that a compound stays in the body before being cleared by the liver or kidneys. Again, drugs that require a single daily dose are almost always superior to those that require more frequent doses, simply because they bring dramatic improvements in patient compliance—patients are far less likely to miss a dose. Obviously, taking the medication as prescribed increases its effectiveness, but, as it turns out, the once-a-day chemistry enhances effectiveness as well. The steady, controlled delivery gives patients more benefit. Alza, one of the original drug delivery companies and among the first to focus on this problem, provides an example of this. Alza developed Pfizer's Procardia, which treats angina (chest pain associated with heart disease), into the once-a-day formulation Procardia XL and demonstrated effectiveness that won its approval for treating not only angina, but high blood pressure as well.

With a refined chemical compound and a carefully selected animal model, a biotech company can see which studies are dead ends and which hold potential. Positive results in this stage bring much of the general excitement about new scientific discoveries. The first publicity about a promising new anticancer compound, for instance, is likely to surface when scientists find that it works in mice. Investors should realize, though, that there is often little correlation between what the media gives attention and what is really significant. Few articles emphasize how long it will be before a drug is likely to reach the market, if it makes it at all. When such comments do appear, they're usually at the end of the article, and readers are apt to ignore them. Scientists have started to adjust for the media's rather simplistic view of their discoveries, recognizing that although the concepts do warrant excitement, it's far too early to know whether they'll lead to a successful drug. Some biotech companies, then, prefer to publicize their findings only once they have shown that a potential drug works in humans.

Obviously, while chances of a drug working in humans are much greater when the preclinical studies are based on a good disease model, even a good animal model has severe limitations. Many of a drug's limitations will only surface later in the drug development process, in human testing. This is especially true when scientists have an incomplete understanding of the specific biological changes that create a disease—the less that is known about the biological changes, the greater the chance of failure in human trials. As the sequencing of the human genome has shown, much of the human system is too complex to correlate to animals. For example, scientists continue to unravel the intricacies of the human immune system, but for now they still must accept unknowns as they work to develop drugs to treat immune system diseases. Drugs to treat sepsis, a complex condition that involves multiple biological pathways, have proven particularly challenging, with multiple failures in late-stage clinical trials.

This is not to say that the information from preclinical studies is worthless for investors. The results here are great indicators of what to watch and, with the right companies and conditions, are potentially good opportunities. I have been following the efforts of a number of companies to find killing agents that can be attached to monoclonal antibodies in order to treat cancer. ImmunoGen, which attaches a potent poison in such a way that the poison is only activated once it is in the cancer cell, saw outstanding results in mice in preclinical studies. The company subsequently signed licensing agreements with monoclonal antibody leaders Genentech and Abgenix and is pursuing its own clinical trials as well, so we should soon know if this technique works as well in humans as it does in mice. I am optimistic.

Besides evaluating a potential drug's effectiveness, preclinical studies also serve to demonstrate whether a drug is safe. Before a drug can progress to human clinical trials, it must pass toxicology studies in animals. The length of the studies and the animals used will vary depending on the drug, the disease, and the intended course of administration. An unusual drug will be subjected to more stringent studies. A drug to treat cancer means fewer safety concerns—it can have severe side effects as long as it works. And a drug for a chronic condition, where the patient may take it for years, demands a longer toxicology study.

Once a company has achieved satisfactory results establishing efficacy and safety—outcomes that materialize in maybe one in a thousand potential drug candidates—it is ready to begin human clinical trials. At this point, it must notify the FDA of its intention to go on to clinical trials by submitting an investigational new drug application (IND). Upon receiving a company's IND, the FDA has thirty days to respond, either by approving the IND and allowing the company to go forward or by asking the company for more information on the preclinical studies results and the intended clinical trials. If the FDA does not respond within the thirty-day period, the company is free to begin Phase I of its clinical trials.

Phase I Clinical Trials

As the first test of a potential drug in humans, the primary objective of a Phase I clinical trials is to verify safety. Initially, healthy volunteers receive a low dose of the drug to see if they tolerate it well, with no harmful side effects. If the drug appears safe, researchers may gradually escalate the dose, continuing to check for adverse reactions.

A good Phase I trial will also provide information on how the drug performs in the body, how much of it appears in the bloodstream, how long it stays in the bloodstream (its half-life), and how the body eliminates it. Typically, a company completes a Phase I clinical trial in less than a year, enrolling thirty to fifty people in the study.

Phase I trials give researchers the first look at whether the potential drug acts differently in animal models than it does in humans. While researchers are seldom surprised when differences arise, they sometimes find conquering these issues more difficult and time-consuming than they would expect. Such a roadblock occurred in the first efforts to gain approval of monoclonal antibodies to treat cancer. The original monoclonal antibodies were made in mice, which worked fine when they were administered to mice. But when they were injected into humans, the human immune systems identified the mouse portion of the injected antibodies as a foreign invader and built up its own antibodies against that portion. This effect worried doctors who saw it in early clinical trials. A number of biotech companies later developed techniques that solved the problem by "humanizing" mouse antibodies, thus greatly reducing the immune system response to them. Further improvements came with the invention of several methods for making fully human antibodies, including the use of transgenic mice.

Sometimes the differences that emerge between mouse and human results are insurmountable. Two naturally occurring human proteins that stimulate the immune system, tumor necrosis factor (TNF) and gamma interferon, generated a lot of excitement as potential cancer treatments when Genentech found great results with them in mice. Amgen saw the opportunity and began testing gamma interferon as well. In human trials, though, neither protein lived up to the early excitement—both showed greater toxicity than expected in the more complicated, less predictable human system (on the flip side, drugs inhibiting TNF have worked in the treatment of rheumatoid arthritis). Large complex human proteins often work very differently in humans than they do in mice, so it is important here to be careful when interpreting the results of preclinical studies. This history later made it easy for me to be cautious in the face of all of the excitement over EntreMed's preclinical antiangiogenesis results using Folkman's famous proteins in mid-1999, results that have yet to show a human correlation.

With some serious diseases, the FDA allows biotech companies to conduct Phase I trials in volunteers who are suffering from the target disease. This gives companies the advantage of obtaining some evidence about possible efficacy—normally a focus of Phase II trials—at an earlier stage. Trials of this nature are sometimes referred to as Phase I/II clinical trials, and they occur either in lieu of or after conventional Phase I trials in healthy volunteers.

In fact, for drugs designed to treat terminal diseases such as cancer, the FDA insists that biotech companies test the drugs in patients who have failed all approved therapies. This policy came in response to the chemotherapy drugs used before biotechnology, almost all of which were selective poisons. The drugs had to show that they played a clear role in increasing survival rates in order to win approval. Although it made sense to treat the sickest patients first, biotech companies found themselves at a disadvantage—the drugs they had designed to stimulate the immune system would obviously work better if the patients' immune systems were still in decent shape. In most very ill cancer patients, prior treatments with radiation and chemotherapy have killed almost all of the white blood cells, destroying the immune system.

This requirement, along with the continued focus on dose escalation, affected the development of one of biotech's earliest biological agents intended to treat cancer, interleukin 2 (IL–2), a human protein that stimulates the immune system. With cancer patients, the historical assumption has been the larger the doses, the more effective the treatment. Trials, then, called for continued dose escalation in patients to determine the maximum tolerated dose. Cetus (now part of Chiron), Amgen, and Immunex all pursued IL–2 treatments, but found that the maximum tolerated dose was not enough to treat cancer. Then, Dr. Steven Rosenberg of the National Cancer Institute found that he could separate a patient's white blood cells, incubate them with IL–2, then put them back into the patient with additional IL–2, creating a way for patients to tolerate higher doses. His success brought a lot of favorable publicity and even landed him on the cover of *Fortune,* but it biased succeeding trials toward higher doses. Of the companies exploring IL–2 treatments, only Cetus had persisted. After failing to gain approval for a version to treat kidney cancer, the company merged into Chiron, which later got IL–2 approved—at a dose that still had serious side effects. Similar factors led to the approval of another early biological agent, alpha interferon, at a dose that carried adverse consequences. Now, years later, doctors are learning that these drugs can be effective at lower doses, especially in combination with other agents.

Biotech companies have also used these drug-testing guidelines for deadly diseases to their advantage. Because of cancer trials' simpler safety criteria, companies that work on gene therapy, first hailed as a means to treat diseases caused by a genetic defect such as cystic fibrosis, now go after cancer. Cancer now accounts for more than half of the current clinical trials using gene therapy. Cancer patients—who are likely to die without radical intervention—are less concerned about the treatment's risks, whereas genetic disease patients would suffer from the occasional side effects they've encountered, sending researchers back for further treatment refinement. Also, because cancer treatment is mostly short-term, companies need not demonstrate long-term safety of the treatment.

Phase II Clinical Trials

Once Phase I trials have proven a potential drug's safety, biotech companies move on to Phase II trials, where they administer the drug to a few hundred patients to determine whether the drug actually works in treating humans and if so, to pinpoint the optimal dosage. Although Phase II trials, which typically take a couple of years, do not prove clinical effectiveness, their design is one of the most important steps of the entire drug development process. Making the best decisions in the design of clinical trials, especially at this phase, can be critical to a biotech company's success.

In designing a Phase II trial, a company must give equal weight to the seemingly contradictory goals of understanding the potential drug as well as possible and finding the quickest way to get the drug approved. Thoroughly understanding the drug will later translate to improved effectiveness, whereas a quick approval may give the company first-to-market advantage and, by shortening the length of the clinical trials, reduce costs. How biotech companies respond to this tension between the need to be careful and the rewards of moving quickly often sets the best companies apart from the others.

Overall, an intelligent and comprehensive Phase II trial program will greatly increase a drug's chances of success in the more expensive

Phase III clinical trials that follow. In their rush to gain approvals, companies sometimes make the mistake of moving on to a Phase III trial without having clearly established the most effective dose. The difference between the right dose and an acceptable dose can result in a marginal trial that makes marketing the drug after approval more difficult or even a failed trial that means backtracking to fix the errors.

Companies sometimes conduct successive Phase II trials to perfect the dose before moving on to Phase III. Cell Genesys, one of the leaders in gene therapy, has promising programs for the treatment of prostate cancer and lung cancer. In both cases, the company takes cancer cells, irradiates them so that they cannot divide, then inserts a gene into them that will produce a granulocyte-macrophage colony stimulating factor (GM-CSF), which stimulates the immune system to attack the cancer. Following encouraging results in its Phase II trials for prostate cancer, the company moved on to test a higher dose. After completing this trial, it will begin a Phase III trial in 2002.

In looking at Phase II trials, it's important to note whether they're conducted according to the same standards that will be imposed on the larger Phase III trials to meet FDA approval. By working to achieve these standards earlier than required, a company improves the design of the Phase III trials, thus enhancing the quality of its results. For most diseases, the Phase III trial should be placebo-controlled and double-blinded.

Placebo-controlled means that some patients in the clinical trial receive the drug being tested and some patients receive a placebo, a chemically inert substance that looks identical to the drug being tested but shouldn't have any effect. Who gets what is determined by the generation of random numbers to ensure against bias, a process called randomization. The patients are "blind," meaning that they don't know whether they're in the experimental group getting the drug or the control group getting the placebo. Placebo control helps companies gauge the impact of the drug against an untreated norm as well as measure what is called the placebo effect. Physicians and psychologists have long noted that many disease patients improve simply because they believe that they are receiving a promising new drug, and growing evidence continues to support this observation. A placebo-controlled trial allows the FDA, as well as the doctors who may someday prescribe the drug, to distinguish between the actual drug effect and the hope instilled simply by participating in an experimental drug trial. Learning the extent of the placebo effect for a particular drug during Phase II is crucial in order to extrapolate to Phase III, where it appears that the effect is even stronger. By accounting for the expected placebo effect during the trial design, companies can be assured of including the number of patients necessary to show statistical significance.

Double-blinded means that both the doctors and patients involved are blind—neither knows which patients are receiving the drug and which patients are receiving the placebo. Sometimes, obvious side effects to a drug make it impossible to blind a trial. In these cases, randomization becomes even more important to prevent bias. Also, doctors from outside the study, whose lack of familiarity with the drug prevents them from knowing which patients are taking it, may be called in to check patients' progress.

Many companies take a shotgun approach to developing drugs, trying to take a number of potential drugs into Phase II trials as quickly as possible. Depending on the drugs and the disease being treated, a company may simultaneously pursue as many as five or six Phase II trials. Amgen serves as the classic example of the wisdom of this approach. When we first recommended its stock in 1985, it had five products either about to start or already in clinical trials. Three of the first four showed little promise and were dropped; the fourth gained approval a few years ago as Infergen and has so far seen only modest sales; and the fifth became the blockbuster Epogen. Later, in the the company's next effort, its sixth drug gained approval as well—Neupogen, with sales of more than $1 billion per year. George Rathmann brought this approach to ICOS too, in his second helmsmanship of a biotech company. Because ICOS focuses on anti-inflammatory products, most of them have the potential to treat a number of diseases. Running multiple tests is helping ICOS find major success.

When a company recognizes that its drug may have the potential to treat a number of diseases, it will conduct multiple Phase II trials to see where the drug works best and what treatment offers the clearest path to approval. In treating cancer, for instance, where the

FDA considers each type of cancer a separate disease, a company can evaluate which type of cancer might facilitate the quickest approval, then weigh this information against the size of that cancer's market. To gain an initial approval, the ideal cancer to target has no current adequate treatment and shows an easily identifiable drug response (as discussed above in relation to gene therapy). With this in mind, many companies are now testing their products in head and neck cancer or pancreatic cancer. The same influences have caused drugs designed to treat excessive inflammation to go on to other targets. Companies have increased these drugs' chances of approval by trying them in concurrent Phase II trials for a number of different diseases, then proceeding with whichever one shows the most promise in terms of both efficacy and time lines.

Phase II results will sometimes indicate a relatively easy path through Phase III trials and on to approval (although a company should never bank on this). In such cases, companies can enhance their Phase III trials with more compelling evidence for the FDA. The Phase II clinical trials that Amgen conducted with kidney dialysis patients with anemia in its development of Epogen, for example, showed such positive results that the company had virtually no doubt that it would have a successful Phase III trial. Amgen added a quality-of-life study to the Phase III trial, examining how many patients were able to return to work during treatment. Showing this broad economic benefit made it easier for the government to later decide to reimburse kidney dialysis patients, who are covered by Medicare, for the cost of Epogen.

Large Phase II trials can occasionally qualify as Phase II/III trials that, if they produce really good results, can be used to file for marketing approval. As with Phase I/II trials, the FDA permits the combined trial in treatments for grave diseases without any effective therapeutics. A variation of this is called a pivotal Phase II trial, in which the FDA sets different rules to allow expedited approvals for drugs that treat life-threatening diseases. The FDA must respond to applications for drugs to treat life-threatening illnesses within six months.

Under expedited approval rules, companies can work toward a different endpoint, the predefined goal against which the results of a trial will be measured. The gold standard of endpoints is the rate of survival. For many years, the FDA insisted on seeing longer survival proven before it would approve new cancer treatments—since almost all cancer treatments had severe side effects, nothing but improved survival rates justified marketing approval. Now, expedited approval rules allow the use of improvements in surrogate markers as endpoints instead. Surrogate markers are conditions that can be measured and are predictive of survival: reduction in the levels of the HIV viral load in AIDS (where the markers were first used) or the number of patients whose tumors show a complete or partial response in cancer (the FDA defines a partial response as a reduction in tumor size of 50 percent or more).

While trials to measure survival might take as long as three years, trials that pursue surrogate marker endpoints can show results in a year. Taxol, approved in 1992, was the first cancer drug to use expedited approval rules. After a treatment has reached a surrogate marker endpoint, however, the rules impose a final condition: The company must have already started or agreed to conduct a conventional Phase III trial that will demonstrate improved patient survival.

Phase III Clinical Trials

By the time a company reaches Phase III trials, it has shown safety in both healthy volunteers and ailing patients as well as efficacy in alleviating disease symptoms or curing disease. The task now is to confirm the safety and efficacy demonstrated in Phase II trials, with the ultimate goal of submitting the results to the FDA to obtain approval to market the drug.

Phase III trials vary greatly in their size and duration, but usually take about three years and involve 1,000 to 3,000 patients (a large enough number to achieve statistically significant results). The longer and larger trial—usually a double-blinded study comparing the potential drug against a placebo or the currently accepted treatment—not only gives confirmation that the drug works, it also provides greater evidence of its safety. Because of their length and size, Phase III trials cost up to $100 million to conduct.

Given this colossal expense, biotech companies are sometimes betting it all on the marketing approval of a drug. Many companies hedge their bets by finding a more affluent marketing partner before beginning their Phase III trials. Some companies have no choice but to take on a partner, as they simply cannot afford to finance a Phase III trial. Others seek partners to make up for a lack of internal clinical trial expertise. In most cases, however, a partnership slows down the drug development process. If the potential market for the drug is narrow enough that the company could reach it single-handedly, the company is better off finding a way to fund the Phase III trial unaided.

The competition between Vertex Pharmaceutical and Agouron Pharmaceutical provides a good demonstration of how a partner can slow the process. The companies were leaders in using X-ray crystallography to reveal proteins' structures, then developing small molecule drugs that stopped the proteins from performing their functions. In the late 1980s, both companies were pursuing a drug to inhibit the protease enzyme, which is necessary for HIV reproduction. Thinking that structure-based drug design was an important technology, I had begun to follow both companies. Vertex, with more sponsorship and twice the market capitalization of Agouron, was better known on Wall Street, partly due to the success of *The Billion Dollar Molecule*, a book that chronicled Vertex's early years.

After reading *The Billion Dollar Molecule*, I became more skeptical about Vertex and its focus on stock price. Then, when Agouron's stock price dipped, we recommended it in the MTSL. A couple of years later, it looked like Vertex had about a year's lead on Agouron in getting the first protease inhibitor to market. Around this time, Vertex signed up Glaxo as a marketing partner to pay for the expensive trials and help with the trial design. Having a partner contributed to a slowdown at Vertex, opening the door for Agouron. Agouron, which understood the importance of speed and hired people with the skills to do the clinical trials properly, got its product, Viracept, on the market almost two years earlier than Vertex's.

Another race for approval is currently under way in the area of antisense, although the competition is not direct, since the companies are targeting different forms of cancer. Both Isis, the leader in the field, and Genta are in Phase III trials using antisense molecules in combination with chemotherapy. Isis is targeting non-small-cell lung cancer, and Genta is working to treat melanoma.

Clearly, this is the phase where trial design will out. If the trial was designed properly to yield the anticipated results, it mostly follows that the FDA will grant approval based on them. In theory, this match-up has become easier in recent years because of the FDA's willingness to discuss clinical trial plans with companies before they begin. In reality, the viewpoints of a company and the FDA are inherently at odds. Serving its concern for clear proof of efficacy and safety, the FDA will always suggest more and larger trials with the most difficult endpoints. Conversely, the company, which already believes in the drug, focuses on how quickly and cheaply it can get the drug approved. Finding the right balance can make a big difference even beyond the sought-after marketing approval, as doctors considering prescribing the drug to patients will often look at the clinical trial's design and scope to evaluate it.

Once the Phase III results are in, the company is ready to file a new drug application (NDA) with the FDA. To be acceptable for approval, the potential drug must show a statistically significant improvement over the placebo or current treatment, which means demonstrating that the probability that the results were due to chance is less than 5 percent. This measure is often expressed as a "p-value," with 0.05 as the cut-off and smaller p-values indicating lower probability that chance produced the improvement shown by the drug.

The FDA can take a year to review the NDA and decide on approvals. Historically, its policies have varied according to its divisions. The drug division, which regulates small molecule drugs, required two Phase III studies to confirm a new drug's effectiveness and safety, whereas the biologicals division, which handles protein- or cell-based therapies (naturally occurring human proteins, monoclonal antibodies, gene therapy, and antisense), would approve new treatments based on one Phase III trial. The rules have since changed, and the drug division will now issue approvals after one Phase III study as well, although a preference for multiple studies remains.

The Big Picture in the Drug Development Process

All told, the drug development process, from idea inception to FDA approval, can take from as few as five to as many as fifteen years. For investors, this means that understanding where a company is in the process and knowing the ramifications of the decisions it makes at each stage are of critical importance. Being aware of the specific traits of different types of drugs is not only important in evaluating a company's pipeline, it also provides some perspectives on the risks of a particular clinical trial and helps in estimating the size of the market for a potential drug.

Use these observations when comparing companies, then look at the market value of each and figure out how much revenue the drugs they're developing will need to produce to make the stock attractive at the current valuation. The risk and reward will change over time for each of these drug types. For monoclonal antibodies, for example, the successes of the last couple of years have significantly lowered the risks associated with making this type of drug. The key questions here now are not whether the potential drug will work but if the company has chosen the right target and what the competition will be by the time the drug is approved and on the market.

Keep in mind, too, that while companies that develop successful drugs to treat prevalent diseases reach huge markets and assure themselves reliable profit streams for years to come, companies that meet failure in clinical trials are perhaps another step closer to a later success, provided they learn from their mistakes.

The Food and Drug Administration

As the arbiter of approvals, the FDA is a major figure on the biotech landscape. When biotech first appeared, the FDA viewed it primarily as a production process, holding a favorable impression of the industry based on its success in the large-scale production of human proteins. When the industry began to develop proteins that had not previously been used in disease treatment, the FDA increased its scrutiny. It looked closely at not only purity and manufacturing controls, but also at these proteins' effectiveness in treating disease. When some human proteins showed toxicity in tests in humans, the FDA became much more careful and, consequently, slower as it evaluated biotech new drug applications.

Like most government bureaucracies, the FDA is very sensitive to statements from both the media and members of Congress. And like most bureaucrats, FDA employees understand that the one action

TABLE 8.1 Drug Development

Discovery	Preclinical	Phase I	Phase II	Phase III
Basic research	Animal studies for safety and desired effects	Safety and dosage in humans	Evaluate effectiveness and toxicity/ side effects in humans	Confirm effectiveness; look for side effects of long-term use

For further information, see www.fda.gov/cder/handbook/develop.htm or www.clinicaltrials.com.

most likely to create controversy is making a decision. These problems are amplified by the fact that the FDA is also protected from criticism—those who are most aware of and likely to complain about the organization's impressionability and unnecessary delays are the very companies that are trying to get drugs approved. Since these companies must continue to deal with the FDA, they bend over backward to not criticize it in any way. Occasionally, a smaller company seeking drug approval forgets this, and the FDA demonstrates the company's mistake by not approving the drug in question. Any news or publicity that reminds people that some drugs in development could cause problems for some of the people who take them serves to exacerbate the FDA's slowness.

The FDA has grown from its 1906 charter to ensure food safety to become primarily concerned with regulating the drug industry (though it also looks at cosmetics, radiation-emitting products, and animal feed and drugs). Since the "wonder drug" era of the mid–twentieth century brought antibiotics and the polio vaccine, the FDA has shown major shifts in its attitude to new treatments, which subsequently affect the attitudes of biotech investors. The FDA's slow bureaucratic tendencies were reinforced in 1960, when Thalidomide, a sleeping drug used to treat morning sickness in pregnant women, was found to cause major birth defects in Europe, South America, Australia, and other places where it had already been approved. The drug was still awaiting approval in the United States, and the media made a hero out of the FDA examiner who

had delayed U.S. approvals. Although the FDA's slowness had a fortuitous effect in this instance, in the long run it probably contributed to the deaths of many Americans who were not able to get
access to beneficial drugs that were slowly winding their way
through the approval process.

In 1988, the AIDS epidemic hit the United States, condemning
patients with the disease to almost certain death without new treatments. These patients caught the attention of the media as they im-
plored the government to speed the FDA process and give them a
chance to live. Their plea resonated with patients suffering from
other diseases as well. The FDA responded to the pressure with new
policies (as mentioned in the discussion of Phase II clinical trials) for
expedited approvals for life-threatening disease treatments and surrogate markers as the basis for initial FDA approval.

These new rules were made law in 1992 with the passage of the
Prescription Drug User Fee Act. This act also required that the FDA
review new drug applications for life-threatening diseases within six
months and others within twelve months. To enable the organization to do this, the act provided for user fees—considerable application fees for submitting a drug for approval—that financed the hir-
ing of new FDA staff. Mean approval times subsequently dropped
from about thirty months prior to the act to around fifteen months
in 2000. During this period, the drug and biotech companies enjoyed predictable response times and patients received new drugs
expeditiously.

Then, in 2000, the FDA recalled several highly visible, previously
approved drugs that, when used by a much larger number of patients than their clinical trials had effectively modeled, caused unexpected side effects. The media picked up the story, a few congress-
men chimed in, and the FDA approval climate changed again.

It worsened further at the start of the Bush administration in
January 2001, when the head of the FDA resigned and Bush did not
immediately nominate a successor (to date, the position is still un-
filled). Without a leader to take responsibility, the FDA bureaucrats
immediately found ways to avoid the intent of the law. At the end
of a drug's yearlong review period, they would send a letter to the
applying company to say that the drug could not be approved until
they received additional information. In some cases this may have

been legitimate, but in most it was just stalling and an unwillingness to make a decision. It's difficult to know which cases were legitimate because no company has been stupid enough to explain to the FDA why it thinks the FDA is wrong and risk even further delays.

Yet the FDA has made positive contributions to streamlining drug approvals, helping to establish uniform drug approval processes around the world. In 1991, it led the creation of the International Conference on Harmonization, which works to coordinate rules in different countries so that companies can use one set of clinical trials for approvals worldwide. There has been some progress since. The European Community established a procedure for filing a marketing application for all of Europe, though after approval a company must still get agreement on prices and reimbursement on a country-by-country basis. Most countries will retain at least some oversight of approvals, as well as modestly different rules. The biggest problems will likely come from Japan, which holds fast to the idea that at least a portion of testing for any drug to be used there must take place in Japan in order to account for its people's unique racial characteristics.

Despite all the times I've found the FDA frustrating, I do believe that it plays a useful role, and I do not agree with proposals to restrict its role to determining safety. Rather, the FDA should make the decision to approve or reject a drug based on a careful consideration of the risks compared to the benefits. The FDA often seems to think that safety is the paramount consideration, but it's not the only consideration. More people undoubtedly die from the lack of a drug whose approval is delayed than from taking an approved drug that later shows serious side effects in a small number of patients.

CHAPTER 9

Patents

While the FDA helps to determine the fates of biotech companies by granting or withholding approvals on new drug applications, another government organization also has a large impact on companies' fortunes: the U.S. Patent and Trademark Office (PTO). In fact, the long drug development process produces much less profit if a company is unable to obtain patent coverage from the PTO. A patent gives its holder exclusive rights to manufacture and market its patented product until the patent expires, protecting it from competition. Considering that as much as fifteen years and $100 million can go into developing a drug, the importance of patent protection is clear.

Some drugs, however, cannot be protected with patents. Human growth hormones, for instance, are an essential drug, but they were not a new discovery. To encourage the development of such drugs, Congress passed the Orphan Drug Act in 1983, providing seven years of exclusive marketing for drugs that serve a patient population of 200,000 or fewer. More than 100 orphan drugs have been approved since.

Investors need to look at patent positions as they evaluate biotech companies, since these exclusive rights are a big part of what makes biotech companies attractive investments. Patents allow companies to profit from their discoveries. Unfortunately, most investors demonstrated ignorance of this fundamental concept in 2000, when they pulled out of biotech stocks because of their justifiably shaken beliefs in Internet stocks. The biotech stocks suffered a backlash based on a comparison that had no validity—both industries included many young companies with bright people and potential for growth, but the Internet industry had no barriers to entry and no patents. (Many companies even had no products, a serious deficiency in their search for profits.) In biotech, formidable financial barriers to entry and strong product patents can give companies an enormous edge over their competitors.

Patents Protect Profits

Year after year, large pharmaceutical companies rank among the most profitable market sectors, in no small part because of patents. Patents are even more important for biotech companies—biotech companies often work on the cutting edge of technology, so their breakthroughs can result in indisputably strong patent positions. The patent system actually encourages such breakthroughs by rewarding their inventors with a period of exclusivity during which they alone can profit from their inventions. Without patents, inventors would have no incentive to share their discoveries, which would keep others from further advancing the state of that particular technology.

To receive a patent, an invention must be new, useful, not obvious, and capable of being reduced to practice, meaning that one can accomplish what it claims. The PTO reviews patent applications to establish that the proposed invention has these qualities, as well as ascertain that the filing party has the right to claim the invention. If two patents covering the same invention are filed within one year, current U.S. practice puts those patents into an interference proceeding, where the PTO determines which party, as the "first to invent," has the right to the claim. In the early years of biotechnology, the PTO did a poor job in this area, allowing some interference proceedings to run for as long as fifteen years before making a decision. It has since improved—it now typically settles interference proceedings within two or three years after an interference is declared and grants straightforward patents within about two years rather than the three to ten years it used to take.

Still, first to invent is a tricky concept. The United States has seen a lot of interesting patent litigation on this issue (no surprise, given the stakes). In the rest of the world, first to invent is simply reduced to first to file—the patent goes to the party that submits the first application for a specific invention. The United States is slowly moving toward adopting a similar approach, as the growing importance of world trade makes patent law conformity across countries more appealing. By ratifying the General Agreement on Trade and Tariffs (GATT) in 1995, the United States took a significant step toward aligning with the rest of the world. Congress continues to resist the change, however, voicing concerns that it would put individual inventors at a disadvantage.

As a result of GATT, the PTO now grants patents for twenty years from the date of filing rather than the previous seventeen years from the date of issue. This extension only applies to patents filed after the PTO instituted the change; some patents filed before 1995 went through long interference proceedings and were finally issued just recently, at which point they received full seventeen-year terms. For these companies, the slow action became a boon, as they now enjoy patent protection longer than any of them would have anticipated.

In biotechnology, variations of design or methodology can create enough differentiation to allow separate patents for the same discovery, but patents often produce a winner-takes-all situation. With this (and the research activities of their competitors) in mind, biotech companies want to establish crystal-clear claims to their products as early as possible. To present a strong first-to-invent case to the PTO and avoid the delays of interference proceedings, biotech companies file patent applications as soon as they identify a promising direction for a potential new drug, in the discovery phase of drug development.

This may seem premature—after all, the potential drug's effectiveness and safety are by no means guaranteed at this stage—but it's one of the most critical steps a company can take. Without the patent, any profits that the drug would ever generate (should it prove viable) would be limited by an earlier onset of competition. Filing so early in the process also allows a twist to biotech patents: repatents. By the time a company receives its patent based on its discovery concept, the product has typically advanced to Phase I or Phase II of clinical trials and undergone adaptations along the way.

By repatenting with a slightly different design or using a different class of patent, the company extends its patent coverage and avoids the unfavorable position of waiting for FDA approval only a few years before its patent expires. If handled properly, patents play a pivotal role in biotech companies' business models, protecting the profits of approved drugs, which in turn fund continued research on new drugs.

Classes of Patents

According to the nature of their discoveries, biotech companies can file for a number of different classes of patents. Each class has its own characteristics, which can affect value. Patents of different classes can also complement one another. Three classes of patents hold the most importance for biotech companies: composition of matter patents, process patents, and patents that cover a specific use of a substance.

Composition of matter patents have been the mainstay of large pharmaceutical companies for years. These patents provide strong protection for a particular chemical entity, preventing other companies from making or using it. As part of the standard practices of not only the pharmaceutical industry but the chemical and other industries as well, composition of matter patents are well understood and rarely leave any openings for competitors to capitalize on. Instead, competitors try to find another way to achieve the effect of the patented substance—pharmaceutical companies direct large portions of their research and development budgets toward finding new chemical entities that perform the same function as a competitor's successful new drug. Often, these are similar to the competitor's drug but fall outside the coverage of the patent. Once Merck showed that its Mevacor lowered cholesterol, for instance, most of the other major pharmaceutical companies set out to develop similar products that were not covered by Merck's patents.

Process patents don't cover any particular substances but rather address a particular way of making a substance. In general, competitors have an easier time getting around process patents, but these patents also offer a means to create a patentable product out of an existing product. Some of the first proteins developed as drugs had been known for years already and thus couldn't be claimed under composition of matter patents; instead, biotech companies won process patents based on the techniques they invented to make the proteins. Companies also use process patents to extend their composition of matter patents, filing for process patents in the later stages of the drug development process. Pharmaceutical companies have become quite aggressive with this practice recently—they have successfully exercised it to keep a generic competitor off the market for a year or two, even if they eventually lose the patent battle.

Patents that cover a specific use of a substance do exactly that— they are function-specific. Under this class of patents, companies can obtain new patents even on substances that have existed for a long time, provided they have found a new use. For example, EntreMed took the discarded sleeping/morning sickness drug Thalidomide and patented it for use in the treatment of cancer through antiangiogenesis. EntreMed subsequently licensed its patents: first to Bristol-Myers, which returned the rights after studying the drug through Phase II clinical trials; then to Celgene, which tried the drug in different areas. Celgene received FDA approval to use Thalidomide to treat leprosy, a chronic disease that damages nerves and skin and leads to severe complications if untreated. The company also found success using Thalidomide "off-label" (permitted for medical purposes, but not FDA-approved for the specific disease) to treat multiple myeloma, a cancer of the bone marrow, and is testing Thalidomide in a number of solid tumors as well. Here, though, the lack of consistent world standards hurts Celgene, as Thalidomide is readily available at lower prices in a number of other countries, including Mexico. Also, as the U.S. patent holder for Thalidomide, EntreMed is entitled to royalties on any profits Celgene realizes from selling it to treat cancer.

The fairly common practice of licensing patents is another area for investors to evaluate. At times, it may seem tricky, since companies enter a variety of licensing agreements. Some companies turn over a patent's potential entirely, choosing to license rather than develop; other companies license their patents while they also pursue the patent's potential themselves. Depending on the strength of the patents and the demand for their intellectual property, companies can sometimes collect more in royalties on a licensed patent used in a number of different products by other companies than they would realize from developing it for a specific product themselves. The area of monoclonal antibodies, for instance, has seen all varieties of licensing agreements. Protein Design Laboratories, founded specifically to develop humanized antibodies, earns modest royalties by licensing its patents to a number of companies. In 2000, the company also signed a cross-license agreement with Genentech, another leader in humanizing antibodies and a pioneer in the therapeutic uses of monoclonal antibodies. Abgenix and Medarex, the two pioneers in developing human antibodies using transgenic mice, have each signed a large number of licensing agreements with both biotech and large pharmaceutical companies as they simultaneously work to develop some monoclonal antibodies on their own.

Misunderstanding Patent Values: Gene Patents

Invariably, biotech companies claim that their patents are extremely valuable. Yet the market value of a patent is often less than its holders assert. Until actual dollar figures start to come in—from sales of a patented product, the wholesale sale of the rights to a patent, or the fees and royalties associated with licensing a patent—patent value is open for interpretation, to varying degrees depending on the nature of the patent.

An area with the widest swings in interpretation is genomics. Wall Street has missed here by not looking beyond the traditional genomics companies. Now that scientists have mapped the entire genome, genomics companies can no longer file patents for genetic sequences, since genetic sequences are no longer new. Instead, companies will win patents when they determine the function of a particular gene and use its associated proteins or other genetic information to create drugs. Good biology, then, will be the key to getting valuable patents in this area. The few genetic sequencing companies that focused on biology early on, such as Millennium Pharmaceuticals, will have an advantage here and are much more likely to end up with valuable patents.

The question remains as to the value of the patents that have already been filed on genetic sequences. Many genomics companies have lots of "patent-pending" discoveries, but until the PTO issues more of these patents and the courts settle a few appeals, we have little idea of how broad and valuable these patents will be. My guess is that those that are issued will have narrow claims once the courts have interpreted them. Even the people who originally filed these patents now agree with this assessment—remember Craig Venter, until recently CEO of Celera, admitting that the Human Genome Sciences patents on partial gene sequences that he heralded as lead scientist on HGS's sequencing efforts are likely to have little value. Besides their diminished patent value, the partial gene sequences, called expressed sequence tags (ESTs), have lost scientific value as well. They served the purpose of locating an entire gene, a function whose value has been superseded by having all of the genes available.

Given the uncertainty surrounding patents on pieces of actual genes, investors should be very careful about buying genomics stocks, even (or especially) those touted by Wall Street as having valuable patents based on the EST patent filings. Going forward, companies will need to not only provide a genetic sequence but also to link that sequence with a function that has medical value in order to win a patent. This means defining the protein the gene produces, along with the protein's biological use.

Although Wall Street has focused on genomics companies, a number of other biotech companies have been doing important work on genes and will more than likely end up with the most valuable patents. Since their inception, these companies have been looking for genes that code for interesting proteins. Genetics Institute, for example, developed a technique for identifying genes that produce proteins that are subsequently secreted by the cells. Since most of the therapeutic proteins sold by biotech companies are secreted proteins, it looked as if the technique would have wide applications. Indeed, Genetics Institute applied its intelligent, systematic method to identify a large number of the associated genes and then offered them to other biotech companies, finding takers in Chiron and Genentech, among others. At the time of this discovery, American Home Products owned 60 percent of Genetics Institute; in 1996, American Home Products acquired the rest of Genetics Institute and has not since discussed the results of this program. Still, Genetics Institute may have patented many of the sequences for secreted proteins, which could not only be valuable but also prevent other companies from protecting their products.

Another smart approach in identifying genes has been to identify the genes expressed in cancer cells. Bristol-Myers started a program along these lines in 2000 and received a lot of good publicity for targeting promising new cancer remedies. What the news coverage ignored, however, was that three years earlier Chiron had recognized the value of this method and entered into a contract with Hyseq to conduct a large similar study, looking at the differential expression of genes in cancers and comparable healthy tissue. So by the time Bristol-Myers identifies any of the genes it's looking for, chances are they'll already be patented as a result of the Chiron-Hyseq study. Wall Street has thus far failed to appreciate this fact, although perhaps it will take notice once Chiron begins clinical trials of potential new cancer drugs based on this genetic information.

As a general rule, it's difficult for any company to get a strong patent position that covers a whole platform technology. This is important for investors to remember, especially when the publicity about a patent may make it seem very broad. In the early days of gene therapy, for example, it seemed that a few patents had the potential to dominate the field. A company called Sandoz (now part of Novartis) paid what I considered outrageous prices to acquire two other companies, Genetic Therapy and Systemix, simply to obtain specific patents that it thought had outstanding potential. In fact, the broad claims of these patents included territory already covered by existing patents. With so many scientists working in all areas of research, the chances of one company ending up with a patent position that covers a broad technology platform are quite small.

A Unique Patent Situation: Antisense

Perhaps the most stunning example of the power of a strong patent position, both in terms of development and licensing, comes in antisense. While the big results in this field still lie ahead, the events of the past ten years have put one company, Isis Pharmaceuticals, in a near-monopoly position.

Antisense prevents the production of proteins implicated in some disease processes by turning off the genes that produce those proteins. It does this by delivering a synthetic piece of genetic code to the gene—when the synthetic genetic code attaches to the target gene sequence, it blocks the body's own genetic components necessary for protein synthesis, stopping the process.

In the 1980s, when antisense first attracted interest, three companies that formed to develop the technology quickly emerged as leaders: Isis, Gilead Sciences, and Hybridon. Investors were excited about antisense's potential to treat any disease caused by the body's excessive production of a specific protein, so the companies were well financed. I remember hearing a Gilead presentation just prior to its IPO and thinking that if all of Gilead's explicit and implicit claims were true, I wouldn't need to listen to any more presentations—using antisense, Gilead was going to cure most human diseases. Of course, antisense proved more difficult to commercialize than people expected (with just one product on the market to date), and Gilead shifted its focus to other areas. In 1999, the company sold its antisense patent portfolio and technology to Isis for $6 million, a fraction of the amount it had invested. In mid-2001, Isis and Hybridon made a deal as well, with Isis paying Hybridon $15 million in cash and other considerations: Hybridon retained the right to continue to develop antisense products using its technology and obtained a nonexclusive license to some of Isis's patents, and Isis got the exclusive right to sublicense Hybridon's patents to others.

Again, despite the slow progress so far, I see great potential in antisense, particularly in treating cancer and inflammatory diseases. Now it seems that any new company that wants to get in on this technology will have to pay royalties to Isis.

Patent Values

Clearly, patents have a large role in making biotechnology a very profitable business, as illustrated by years of competition-free, profitable sales for almost every biotech company with products on the market. Yet neither the media nor the Wall Street analysts do a good job of discussing patents, instead accepting a company's claims of its patent values with little thought or investigation.

A company will always assert the strength of its patents. Some of these assertions are valid but others are inflated claims, part of a company's conscious effort to gain an advantage by convincing investors and competitors of its superior patent position. These claims may keep competitors from developing products around the murky edges of a patent's intellectual property rights—a nice outcome, since intimidating a competitor with hubris early on costs much less than prosecuting it later. Investors, then, should be skeptical, not only to account for the company's exaggeration but also because the value of a specific patent is inherently unpredictable. Often, investors must look further to make estimates of a patent's value.

The best information on the real value of patents comes from a company's competitors and licensees. Both of these groups will have examined the patents in detail. Competitors need to know how the other company accomplishes their shared objective, whether to gain information about how other approaches play out, seek opportunities for adaptation, or find out if patent infringement is occurring in either direction. Licensees need to assess the technology they intend to use, in terms of both scientific and monetary value, before entering agreements. I do not always concur with the competitors' ultimate assessments, but their comments help define the important issues.

Investors can do additional, primary legwork to determine a patent's value. Many people think of patents as the complicated domain of specialized attorneys, but I contend that having an awareness of what is happening in a field goes further than legal training in understanding the value of a patent. If a patent holds great importance for an individual company, it's worth reading the document itself rather than relying on an interpretation. A good patent will state its claims in clear language, so any reader with some knowledge of the science should be able to gauge its importance. The key points to keep in mind are what the patents cover and whether they provide the company with real protection from potential competitors. Also, never mistake quantity for quality—the question is not the number of patents a company has, but what those patents cover and provide.

As much as patent holders hope to avoid them, court cases are a normal part of the patent process. If there is a big enough profit potential, even strong patents will suffer infringement. For example, Chiron's patent on hepatitis C diagnostics based on its 1986 discovery of the hepatitis C virus seemed unassailable. Yet lured by the large market potential and emboldened by the well-known limitations of diagnostic patents (it's often easy to work around them by finding another way to do the same thing), many companies pursued Chiron's work. Chiron tried to enforce the patents, spending years in litigation with companies that, based on their own strong positions in diagnostics, were willing to spend a lot of money to overturn the Chiron patent. Only after suffering a number of court losses did Hoffman–La Roche, the biggest predator, finally settle at the end of 2000, paying $85 million for the hepatitis C virus portion plus substantial royalties of about $30 million a year. Chiron collected on one of the big values of leading science—it produces strong patents, which result in profits from either well-protected products or royalties from other companies or both.

Court cases such as this define much of patent law, especially in a new area such as biotechnology. In fact, the decisions of the Federal Circuit Court of Appeals in Washington, D.C., have built the bulk of recent patent law, for two reasons. First, the Supreme Court hears very few patent cases and thus sets very little patent law. Second, since 1984, all trial cases on patents that advance to appeals have gone directly to this particular court of appeals. This court of appeals, whose judges include a number of former patent attorneys, demonstrates a clear propatent bias, which has increased the value of patents. Clearer court decisions, a result of a 1996 Supreme Court ruling that judges rather than jurors should decide patent claims, have improved the enforcement of patents and added to their value as well.

Over the years, I have read a number of patents that were being contested and have found that the appeals court almost always takes a rational point of view that aligns with the patent language. Seeing this pattern can provide investors with opportunity, dramatically illustrated in a battle between Amgen and Genetics Institute over recombinant erythropoietin (EPO), Amgen's Epogen. Amgen had lost at the trial court level, unable to convince the court that Genetics Institute had infringed on Amgen's patent. But in March 1991, the court of appeals ruled in Amgen's favor. Amgen's stock jumped more than 20 points, gaining $1 billion in market value. While this seemed like a lot of money at the time, it pales in comparison to the future earnings that the ruling protected. I estimate that half of Amgen's $70 billion in current market capitalization can be attributed to its sales of Epogen and the royalties from Johnson & Johnson's sales of Epogen for other uses and in other markets. Just as Amgen profited enormously from this court of appeals decision, investors who appreciated the value of Amgen's patent could have profited as well.

By asking and answering the right questions, individual investors can make intelligent judgments about the value of a company's patents. Then they can assess how that value affects the value of the company as a whole, relating the patent to the potential for specific products and examining what competing companies are doing. While interpreting patents will remain an area of some risk, the investor who makes the effort to analyze their value can gain an edge.

CHAPTER 10

Looking at Deals:
IPOs, Partnerships, and
Mergers and Acquisitions

As financial vehicles, biotech companies are entering a new stage in their development. Certainly, some of the old rules apply: Their ability to raise money can be affected by sector- and marketwide cycles, and the Achilles' heel of their business model—promising products carrying the risk of failure in testing and in the marketplace—remains the same. But after a quarter-century of using public funds to research and launch products, biotech companies have repeatedly demonstrated their ability to create effective, profitable drugs. This track record of success has given biotech companies more leverage in negotiating all kinds of deals, and with the experience gained from the passage of time, biotech companies know what to do with their improved negotiating position. Partnerships are proliferating and taking on new and interesting characteristics. Mergers and acquisitions are also on the rise, generally as a result of large biotech companies combining with or snapping up smaller biotech companies. And while IPOs remain a cyclical phenomenon within the industry, the unprecedented influx of cash from Wall Street's financing of the IPO classes of late 1999 and 2000 is one of the main forces behind the current escalation in deal making.

Money may be fueling this burst of activity, but what's driving these deals is a simple business problem: Some biotech companies have too much cash, others have too much product. This in itself isn't a new development but what's interesting is how the recent huge inflows of capital have affected the parties involved in the current spate of deals. It's important to keep in mind that in the wake of the 1999–2000 financing boom, "cash-rich" and "cash-poor" are relative terms. Cash-rich companies may have what would historically have been considered healthy product pipelines, but in the current environment they don't have enough in development to justify either their current financial position or their stock valuation. The need for product has spurred them to hunt for cash-poor companies that have been able to finance the development of multiple products (thanks to the financing boom) to the point where the scope of what they're doing is more than they can manage in-house, driving them to seek out partners, collaborators, licensers, or even acquirers.

It's my belief that the heightened level of deal-making activity we've seen across the last year or so is likely to continue for some time—there are still many large biotech companies and pharmaceutical companies hungry for products to accelerate future growth in sales and profits. In addition, the industry's latest arrivals—the genomics companies—are moving from selling information to developing their own products, which means they're transitioning into the most competitive segment of biotech, setting the stage for more mergers and acquisitions.

In aggregate, the effect of the current and imminent deals on the industry will be substantial. Large biotech companies and medium-size pharmaceutical companies will subsume smaller biotech companies, creating a void that will be filled by a new round of small biotech companies. Partnerships inside and outside the industry will continue to grow more sophisticated, with biotech companies retaining more of the value in the agreements than they ever have before. In individual cases, the emergence and outcomes of deals are obviously impossible to predict; in fact, it's difficult to construct a general set of rules by which an individual investor can evaluate IPOs, partnerships, mergers, and acquisitions. However, by taking a closer look at the structure of recent examples of each of these financial arrangements, the individual investor can learn what to look for and which questions to ask when assessing the merits of deals.

Initial Public Offerings (IPOs)
and Secondary Offerings

The initial public offering (IPO) and its cousin, the secondary offering, are rights of passage in biotechnology, signaling the final transition of a start-up out of the laboratory and into the business arena. The money that biotech companies raise from the public gives them the flexibility and staying power that are critical to long-term success. Although the history of the sector is brief, the pattern is for the public markets to take a heightened interest in financing biotech IPOs roughly every four years, with the most recent concentrated bursts of IPO activity coming in 1995–1996 and late 1999–2000.

The latter of these booms is likely to be remembered as the moment in which biotech financially came of age. It began with an explosion in financing outside the sector (most notably in high-technology and Internet companies, including dot-coms), the effects of which then spread to biotechnology in late 1999 as genomics companies began to attract attention, creating the best IPO financing window the industry has ever seen. Biotech companies raised record-breaking levels of capital in 2000, more than tripling the amount of money drawn into the industry in 1999 from selling securities. When compared to the last truly critical financing cycle in biotechnology's short history (1991–1992), the stature of the 2000 boom only increases. In the peak month (January) of the 1991–1992 boom, the industry raised $754 million, a figure that was dwarfed by the 2000 boom's top month (February), in which it drew in $6 billion.

The IPO class of 2000 trumps its 1995–1996 counterpart in terms of average postdeal valuation as well. The 1995–1996 group, heavily weighted toward combinatorial chemistry companies (the hot new tools companies of that period), generated an average postdeal valuation of $110 million. Meanwhile, the IPOs of 2000, featuring the debuts of genomics, bioinformatics, and DNA chip companies, weighed in with an average valuation of $409 million.

The wave of capital from the 2000 boom broke broadly across the industry, and the dramatic inflow of cash has provided many biotech companies with the flexibility to both develop broad pipelines and retain product rights further into the development cycle. The likely end result: Biotech managers will have real opportunities to leverage these robust product pipelines to build significantly more valuable companies. In this way, the fund-raising success of 2000 has fundamentally strengthened the industry.

Across the past twenty years, I've all too often seen cash-strapped biotech companies cede the lion's share of product revenues to large pharmaceutical companies in exchange for measly milestone payments and mediocre royalty agreements. I'm excited by the fact that the recent influx of capital should make this kind of financial concession a rare occurrence. It's one of the reasons I look past the media's excitement in the science of genomics and stem cell technology and point to 2000's record inflows of capital as that year's single most important development in the biotech industry. And it's also one of the factors that contributes heavily to my belief that biotech stocks will be the single best sector to invest in across the next five to ten years. For the first time, the industry has the ability to develop cutting-edge drugs unobstructed by the demands and restrictions of conservative (and sometimes even stingy) corporate partners. In short, the presence of adequate levels of cash both decreases the risk and increases the upside potential for individual biotech companies.

That said, while an initial public offering always attracts my interest, over time I've learned that the moment of a company's IPO doesn't necessarily signal an opportune time to invest in its stock. The 2000 boom may have bolstered the financials of newer, smaller biotech companies, but it's also driven them to higher market caps, leaving less on the table for the individual investor. Given the high market caps of recent IPO companies and the inherently long development time lines in drug development, investors would do well to watch and wait for better opportunities to put money into the newest biotech companies. Their patience might be helped by the knowledge that throughout biotech's twenty-year public history, the vast majority of IPOs have sold below their opening prices within their second year of trading publicly, giving patient investors some very attractive entry points.

Secondary Offerings

A secondary offering is a financing vehicle by which a company that has already gone public enlists a banker to sell new shares of its stock. As a financing vehicle, the secondary offering has two main benefits. The first, of course, is the cash it generates—like an IPO, it's one of the best and fastest ways to raise money. The second benefit is a bit more subtle: Through a combination of visibility from the road show (a series of meetings with potential investors, conducted by a company and its underwriter to stimulate interest in the offering) and the resulting sponsorship from the investment bank's analyst, the stock is likely to attract a broader group of investors.

How the stock price of a biotech company reacts to the announcement of a secondary stock offering depends on the market climate. For most companies in 2000, announcements of secondary offerings resulted in stock price advances. An influx of cash in the bank, exposure from the road shows, and bullish reports written by the analysts for the firms leading the stock offerings triggered these rises. In poor biotech markets, secondary offerings usually result in modest drops in stock prices. Then, depending on how well the management does in telling the company's story and how well the underwriters do in selling and placing the stock, stock prices will either move up or remain stuck in the original price range until further notice. Thus, the price action of stocks after secondary offerings provides a good gauge of how investors feel about the sector in general.

Partly as a result of the sponsorship (that is, the number of analysts following the stock) that comes from raising money, the biotech companies with the largest amounts of cash have tended to sell at higher valuations. I recognize that more cash does reduce the risk, but the higher valuations also make these stocks less attractive investments. In recent times, companies in this high-valuation category included Gilead Sciences, Protein Design Labs, and genomics companies such as Human Genome Sciences and Millennium.

Given these examples, it doesn't make sense to pursue a strategy of investing in biotech companies in anticipation of secondary offerings. Investors are better off picking companies based on value, and then later enjoying an additional, unexpected boost from a well-executed secondary offering. Some of the most successful biotech investments are to be found among companies that move from making scientific progress to increasing valuations to attracting more analysts to raising more money via secondary offerings. When companies run this gamut, their valuations can move up dramatically.

For example, we recommended ImClone Systems in the *Medical Technology Stock Letter* in January 1998 at a price of $3.06 (adjusted for splits). A year later, the stock was up modestly to $5 a share. Then investors began to recognize that the company's lead drug would be on the market within a couple of years, and by January 2000 the stock was at $30 on its way to a high of $85 in the wild market of 2000. Along the way, the company raised $94 million from a secondary offering in November 1999 and an additional $240 million from the sale of convertible debentures in February 2000. The November 1999 offering was fortuitously timed for ImClone, accelerating a price advance that had begun shortly before the fund-raising effort.

A Word on Dilution

Any time a company sells stock, it reduces the fractional ownership of the current shareholders—an event called "dilution." In the short term, dilution can have a negative effect on a company's stock price. However, given the long time lines and the incremental progress in drug development, it makes sense that biotech companies raise capital in a stepwise manner through additional offerings as they show proof of their ability to develop their pipelines. Thus, dilution may hurt in the short term, but without the capital, companies would be forced to give away their future to pay current bills. A sign that the industry is maturing is that companies with late-stage products can raise capital easily in today's environment. This is the result of investors anticipating the near-term revenues of late-stage products before they hit the market.

Partnerships

In biotech, the forms of partnership are the same as those found in any other industry. Alliances, collaborations, and marketing agreements populate the sector, serving as conduits for marketing expertise, technology validation, and money. Their influence over the industry appears to be increasing; each passing year brings new records for the aggregate number of deals struck per annum and the average size per deal. This steady growth has brought changes in how the industry approaches partnerships—although small biotech companies continue to gravitate toward large pharmaceuticals to forge agreements, the real boom in partnership agreements is between small biotech companies and either larger biotech companies or medium-size pharmaceuticals. The industry is now producing roughly 200 partnerships between two or more biotech companies each year, and the volume and the pace of these types of deals are likely to grow.

The frequency and complexity of the new biotech partnership agreements can be mind-boggling, even with respect to a single company. Consider, for example, the Elan Corporation. Based in Ireland, Elan started as a drug-delivery company and has since aggressively expanded from that base to create a web of 223 alliances. These include a number of Elan's acquisitions of biotech companies, Athena Neuroscience, Neurex, and the Liposome Company among them. But the most interesting feature is Elan's approach to structuring alliances with biotech companies. The typical deal is built up from a joint venture to develop a specific product or technology. To fund the partner's portion of the joint venture, Elan typically buys either the partner's stock (at a premium to the current market price) or convertible notes. To prevent the transaction from hurting Elan's current earnings, the company also includes a license to some of Elan's drug delivery technology, which Elan can book as current earnings. Elan has twenty-five such alliances, and a number of them feature interesting products from excellent companies. The joint venture structure of the deals allows the biotech companies to retain half of the profits from their dealings with Elan, and Elan's equity positions allow it to participate in the potential of other products in its partners' pipelines.

Elan's maze of partnerships is a long way from where biotech's original collaborations began. The industry's first partnerships typically featured biotech companies collaborating with large pharmaceutical companies. Because they were product focused, the deals were usually based on straight royalty agreements. The biotech companies would research and identify products and then license them to the pharmaceutical companies, who took responsibility for the clinical development and marketing. In the early days, the royalty rate typically fell between 5 and 7 percent of sales, a range dictated by the large pharmaceutical companies. During this period, biotech companies didn't have the track record they have now; there was a lot of pressure on them to make deals simply to validate their technologies. Linking up with large pharmaceutical companies gave biotech companies a sort of stamp of approval for their product development efforts, the kind that could attract the attention of Wall Street and lead to initial public offerings.

Gradually, the deals got better for the biotech companies. The more they brought products to market, the less important the need for large pharmaceutical company ties became, enabling biotech companies to negotiate more favorable terms in their partnerships. Biotech company managers also simply grew savvier with experience, learning to increase their negotiating leverage by courting multiple partners and getting them to bid against each other for the rights to market and license a single product.

One of the early deals that signaled biotech's newfound increase in bargaining power was the agreement reached between Amgen and Johnson & Johnson for EPO/Epogen in 1985. Johnson & Johnson adopted a typically tough negotiating stance, insisting that the royalty remain in the normal 5 to 7 percent range. But the arrangement Johnson & Johnson settled on allowed Amgen to retain the right to market Epogen in the United States to patients who were undergoing kidney dialysis treatments. Amgen pushed for this concession because it believed that it could go after a focused market using in-house resources, rather than seeking out assistance from large pharmaceutical companies for each and every product when it reached the marketing stage. The insight that different products require marketing efforts of different scales and scopes was a breakthrough in the biotech industry. Today, Amgen continues to market Epogen with great skill—2001 revenues for that product alone exceeded $2 billion.

Another breakthrough in terms came when Chiron negotiated a joint blood screening deal with the Ortho division of Johnson & Johnson in 1985. Instead of licensing its expertise about HIV or developing a product itself, Chiron formed a joint venture under which the two companies split the profits. Ortho provided money up front to fund the research along with marketing skills at the back end when the product was ready to be marketed, and Chiron conducted the research and provided the critical technology on which the product was based. This venture prospered with Chiron's addition of the rights to blood screening for hepatitis C and, in recent years, has provided Chiron about $80 million a year in pretax profits.

So over the past twenty-five years, the quality of partnerships has improved for biotech companies. Historically, the driver for this trend has been the industry's growing reputation for bringing effective products to market. Currently, biotech companies are negotiating partnerships with favorable terms because of the increased pressure on pharmaceutical (and larger biotech) companies to continue to grow rapidly, even as existing products come off patent and encounter generic competition that reduces revenues. The question is: What can an individual investor do to take advantage of these trends in partnerships?

While it's valuable to know what's happening in aggregate, the real prize—using general principles to evaluate specific deals—is elusive. There are too many variables involved in biotech partnerships and too much unreported, misunderstood, or unquantifiable data to lift broadly applicable principles out of individual cases. For example, it's generally known that the average size of product deals is increasing, but it's hard to quantify the terms of any given deal, since the details of most partnership agreements are never fully disclosed to the public. This level of secrecy makes life difficult for investors, but then, when it comes to partnerships, so does publicity.

Generally speaking, loudly publicized deals featuring large dollar figures and catchy headlines have a bigger impact on stock prices than partnerships struck outside of the spotlight, regardless of the actual merit of the deals in question. Sometimes the headline-grabbing numbers featured in a deal look downright modest and uninteresting on closer inspection. When Guilford Pharmaceutical announced a major agreement with Amgen in August 1997 for the development of Guilford's neuroimmunophilin ligands, the media touted it as a $465 million deal. In reality, the agreement broke down into less impressive components—there was a $15 million cash payment, a $15 million stock purchase, a $5 million purchase of warrants, and a $13.5 million research investment spread over three years. The remaining $392 million of the original $465 million would only be paid in full if all ten of

Guilford's potential disease targets included in the agreement resulted in approved products for Amgen—an unlikely goal which, even if realized, would take at least ten years to attain. At the time of the deal, I focused only on the cash payment and the research funding (a surefire total of $28.5 million) when evaluating the agreement. As it turns out, the agreement was terminated in September 2001, with only one of the products reaching human clinical trials, where it produced disappointing results.

Given the level of complexity in modern biotech partnerships, perhaps the best approach for investors is to look at arrangements from the perspective of biotech corporate management. Each deal may be unique, but there's some merit in understanding what the companies are hoping will result from each arrangement and grasping the questions they must have run through before forging each partnership.

A biotech company has much to consider before it even begins conversations with prospective partner companies. First, it has to look at its end of the offer: Is it coming to the table with a technology, or merely a promising research lead on a possible technology? If it has a number of products in the pipeline, the biotech company may not have the people or the money to develop all of the products on its own. Once the company has decided where the technology ranks within its pipeline (What stage of development is it in? What is its revenue potential?), the company has to begin to imagine what kind of deal it wishes to pursue.

The answer to this question may depend on what kind of company the biotech is. If it's a company that's in the business of providing tools to help other companies develop drugs, its approach may be to strike a large number of small deals with a broad array of companies, both to spread risk and to enlarge market share. For example, Incyte, a leading supplier of genomics information, has licenses with most of the large pharmaceutical companies, more than fifty biotech companies, and more than 1,000 research institutions, the sum of which generated more than $200 million in revenues in 2001. These licenses vary significantly in their annual fees depending on their scope and the type of partner. They also contain provisions for royalties should any of the partners develop products using Incyte's genomics information.

On the other hand, recent industry developments have opened the way for tools companies to take the opposite approach in hammering out deals—it's now possible to forgo the small deals, many nonexclusive partners strategy in favor of agreeing to larger, more exclusive deals with a handful of companies. This new approach has been made possible over the last few years by the desire of many drug companies to enhance their own abilities in drug discovery by bringing capabilities for combinatorial chemistry and genomics in-house. In contrast to Incyte, the genomics company Human Genome Sciences signed an exclusive deal with SmithKline (now part of Glaxo) for $125 million at its inception. The advent of these types of deals brings the age-old trade-off of money now versus money later into the arena of tools companies. Technology deals offer the attraction of near-term cash, but they come at the expense of a partial loss of potentially larger long-term profits to be had when products reach the market and royalties kick in.

If the biotech company is a drug (rather than a tools) company, it will face layered issues of scope, timing, and resource allocation with respect to any deal it's considering. In other words, the biotech company must decide at what stage of development the deal should be done as well as whether related products should be included in the agreement. When a product-oriented deal is made at an early stage, it usually has a disease focus and includes all of the potential products to treat that disease. However, as drug discovery gets more sophisticated, the deal may be focused on specific intervention points. For example, Isis Pharmaceuticals' deal with Boehringer Ingelheim was limited to drugs that interfere with ICAM–1, a molecule that controls the way white blood cells exit the blood vessel into tissue at the point of inflammation. The specificity of this agreement left Isis with the freedom to independently pursue many other inflammation targets outside the scope of the agreement.

In addition to determining the scope of any partnership, the biotech company needs to decide at which point during the product's development cycle a deal makes the most sense. While it's generally true that the further along a product is in development, the more it should be worth, this is not a linear progression. Sometimes a potential partner is excited about a specific approach and is willing to pay a good price early; in these cases, the only reason to delay is if the biotech company is considering marketing the product using in-house resources. Most of the time, however, the biggest profits result from signing on with a marketing partner as the product nears approval. In these cases, the price of the long-term profit potential is paid up-front—the biotech company incurs all the precommercialization costs and development risk on its own. Cor Therapeutics, for example, retained marketing rights of its lead product Integrilin until just before it anticipated receiving approval. In 1995, Cor signed an agreement with Schering-Plough for the comarketing and promotion of Integrilin, allowing Cor to share equally in U.S. profits. The timing of the agreement turned out to be unexpectedly fortunate for Cor when the FDA delayed approval of the drug. Because of the partnership, Cor had ample cash to continue normal operations while waiting for the final approval, which came in the first half of 1998. With Integrilin approved and generating profits, Cor became an attractive acquisition target and was recently purchased by Millennium.

The timing and execution of these types of decisions are difficult for a biotech, but in the current environment there's a way for a biotech company to hedge its bets. If a company has a healthy pipeline of drugs in development, it can manage its potential products like a portfolio. It can earmark one or more products for immediate licensing agreements to cover development costs. Meanwhile, it can hold off on partnership agreements for products that may need large sales forces to market, waiting until Phase II clinical trials show that they have a chance of making it to the marketplace. The company can also take certain products off the negotiating table—specifically, niche products that can be marketed by small sales forces managed in-house.

Ligand Pharmaceuticals provides a good example of how a biotech company can develop partnering strategies by managing its pipeline like a portfolio. The company has separated its lines of business into two divisions—one for large-market products requiring large sales forces, one for niche products. The first, Ligand Corporate Partner Products, is responsible for the development of products with potential markets large enough to make marketing partnerships a necessity. The division oversees products licensed to drug companies such as Pfizer, American Home Products, and Eli Lilly, addressing sizable markets such as osteoporosis, cardiovascular disease, and diabetes, all of which require large sales forces to serve. Partnerships created in this division typically call for the partner to bankroll research and assume responsibility for clinical development and marketing. The agreements usually feature milestone payments and royalties ranging from 6 to 15 percent. Ligand's second division, Specialty Pharmaceutical Products, focuses on cancer and dermatology. It boasts four approved products, with a fifth waiting in the wings for FDA approval. All of these products have been approved initially for small market opportunities, but are being tested for much larger related markets.

The one problem here is that Wall Street has not been excited, at least in part because Ligand is a complicated company, and also because analysts have preferred to focus on the approved products, largely ignoring the considerable potential of the products being developed by Ligand's partners. Two of these products, one by Pfizer and one by American Home Products, are now in Phase III trials for osteoporosis. Both of these products use Ligand's selective estrogen receptor modulator (SERM) technology. Ligand is the leader in this technology, and both of these products have the potential to generate revenues in excess of $1 billion—still, Wall Street is only just beginning to sit up and take notice.

The final portfolio strategy for a biotech company to consider isn't product-based, but rather tactical: Namely, the biotech company must determine the geographical reach of each partnership agreement. Although most large pharmaceutical companies would prefer to have worldwide rights to each product, they're not always willing to pay as much as this justifies. The potential pharmaceutical company partner may have a limited position in some foreign countries where the opportunity is large. ImClone Systems, for instance, has taken advantage of such opportunities abroad in its partnership negotiations. While ImClone was developing its lead product, Erbitux, on its own in the United States and Canada, the company generated a significant amount of cash by licensing European rights to Merck KgaA, an agreement it reached after announcing excellent Phase II trial results for Erbitux (when combined with radiation) in the treatment of head and neck cancer. ImClone also has an agreement with Merck KgaA for the licensing of BEC2, a cancer vaccine designed to prevent the recurrence of small-cell lung cancer after surgery. BEC2 has yet to be approved; it will likely take longer to move through clinical trials than Erbitux, and if it is ever approved, the drug will serve a far smaller market. Knowing this, ImClone sought out Merck KgaA to fund the clinical trials, while retaining the right to comarket BEC2 in the United States. The advantage of this approach was demonstrated in September 2001, when just prior to filing for FDA approval, ImClone signed a very large marketing deal with Bristol-Myers for Erbitux.

As in the case of a tools company, the conflict between money now and money later lies beneath most of the partnership questions a biotech drug company must face. The more limited a biotech's financial resources are, the more it will emphasize immediate fundraising over far-off potential profits. But demanding more up front in the way of licensing fees ensures much tougher negotiations for milestone payments and royalties.

Mergers and Acquisitions

In the early days of biotech, industry experts speculated that the trend in merger and acquisition activity would result in biotech companies being subsumed by much larger pharmaceutical companies. It seemed that the speculation was validated in 1985, when Eli Lilly announced the acquisition of Hybritech, a San Diego biotech company focused on monoclonal antibodies. Lilly's announcement led to Bristol-Myers acquiring another biotech, Seattle-based Genetic Systems. The scientific and market potential of monoclonal antibodies to treat cancer were the primary drivers of these deals, and in the ensuing years some of this potential has been realized. Monoclonal antibodies that treat cancer (such as Herceptin and Rituxan) have fueled some of the biotech sector's recent impressive growth, but the expert predictions of large pharmaceutical companies swallowing the biotech industry whole never came to pass. The Hybritech and Genetic Systems acquisitions didn't pan out—many of the key employees left and the drugs in their pipelines never materialized.

As a result, the next agreements between pharmaceutical companies and biotech companies were acquisitions of a controlling interest

rather than of the entire company, a method of preserving the entrepreneurial spirit that resulted in retaining key people. Genentech and
Roche, Immunex and American Cyanamid (Lederle, now part of
American Home Products), Genetics Institute and American Home
Products, and Ciba-Geigy (now Novartis) and Chiron were the high
profile deals. Although these deals worked out better for large pharmaceutical companies than their first attempts at acquiring biotech
companies, the partial buyouts featured options for buying the rest of
the biotech companies at fixed prices, features that contributed to
long slumps in the prices of partially acquired biotech companies'
stocks. (Chiron avoided this problem by selling only 49 percent and
leaving any subsequent acquisition to be negotiated later.) Having
taken their lumps within the biotech industry, large pharmaceutical
companies continue to make acquisitions, but they do so far more
rarely and selectively than had been anticipated—witness Johnson &
Johnson's acquisition of Centocor, or Warner Lambert's (now Pfizer's)
purchase of Agouron. Interestingly, these large pharmaceutical companies pursued their targets only after the biotech companies had
successful drugs on the market—an expensive time to buy.

Though large pharmaceutical companies' acquisitions of biotech
companies still command headlines from time to time, the real action
in biotech deals is taking place elsewhere. During the last couple of
years, the pace and volume of biotech mergers and acquisitions have
increased. Much of the activity has come as the result of intraindustry
maneuvers—larger biotech companies have been buying smaller
biotech companies, transactions that have been fueled for the most
part by the money raised during the 2000 financing cycle. While it's
hard to say whether—in the words of a number of industry analysts—there are "too many" biotech companies, I believe it's safer and
more accurate to claim that the industry suffers from a shortage of
biotech managers who can navigate companies to profitability. As
such, the trend of companies with exciting technologies but flawed
business models being snapped up by better-financed (and often bet-
ter-run) companies is likely to continue for some time to come. The
sizable sums of cash brought into the industry by the 2000 financing
boom will now allow larger biotech companies to compete with large
pharmaceutical companies for prime acquisitions.

TABLE 10.1
Big Pharmaceutical Companies Acquiring Biotech Companies

Biotech co.	Acquirer	Date	Deal (millions)
DNAZ Research Institute*	Schering-Plough	1982	$30
Agrigenetics*	Lubrizol	1983	N/A
Hybritech	Eli Lilly & Co.	1985	$375
Genetic Systems	Bristol-Myers	1985	$294
Zymogenetics*	Novo Nordisk	1988	$NA
Sungene*	Lubrizol	1989	$ND
Damon Biotech	Abbott Labs	1989	$9
Praxis Biologics	American Cyanamid (now part of AHP)	1989	$237
Gen-Probe	Chugai Pharmaceutical	1989	$110
Triton Biosciences*	Schering AG	1990	N/A
Codon*	Schering AG	1990	N/A
Genentech	Roche Holding	1990 6/99	$2.1B for 60% Full acquisition
Immunex	American Home Products	3/93	$600 for 54.6% stake
Genetics Institute	American Home Products	1/92	60% stake for $666
Systemix Inc.	Novartis AG	2/92 2/97	60% for $392 40% for $75.6
Applied Biosystems	Perkin-Elmer Corp.	2/93	$330
Sphinx Pharma*	Eli Lilly & Co.	9/94	$75
Selectide Corp.*	Marion Merrell Dow (now Hoechst Marion Roussel)	1/95	$58
Chiron Corp.	Ciba-Geigy (now Novartis)	1/95	$2,100 for 49.9% stake
Affymax NV	Glaxo	3/95	$539
Genetic Therapy Inc.	Novartis AG (Sandoz)	8/95	$295
Applied Immune Sciences Inc.	Rhône-Poulenc Rorer	12/95	$84.9
Mycogen Corp.	DowElanco	2/96, 12/96	$239 for 52% stake
Canji Corp.*	Schering-Plough Corp.	2/96	$54.5

(continues)

TABLE 10.1 *(continued)*

Biotech co.	Acquirer	Date	Deal (millions)
Calgene Inc.	Monsanto Co.	3/96, 11/96	$250 for 55% stake
Trophix Inc.*	Perkin-Elmer Co.	5/96	N/A
Agracetus Inc.	Monsanto Co.	5/96	$150
Athena Neurosciences	Elan Corp. plc	6/96	$635
Genetics Institute Inc.	American Home Products	12/96	$1,000 for remaining 40%
GenScope Inc.*	Perkin-Elmer Corp.	2/97	NA
Calgene Inc.	Monsanto Co.	5/97	$240 for rest of co.
Perceptive Biosystems Inc.	Perkin-Elmer Corp.	1/98	$360
Sano Corp.	Elan Corp. plc	3/98	$392.8
Apollon Inc.*	American Home Products	5/98	N/A
Gene/Networks*	Warner-Lambert	5/98	N/A
Somatogen Inc.	Baxter International Inc.	5/98	$189
Neurex	Elan Corp. plc	8/98	$740
Penederm Inc.	Mylan Labs	10/98	$205
Sequus Pharma. Inc.	Alza Corp.	10/98	$580
Nanosystems	Elan Corp. plc	10/98	$150
Mycogen Corp.	Dow AgroSciences	11/98	$411.6
DeKalb Genetics Corp.	Monsanto Co.	12/98	$3,700
TheraTech Inc.	Watson Pharma. Inc.	1/99	$300
Depotech Corp.	Skyepharma plc	3/99	$55.7
Agouron	Warner-Lambert	5/99	$2,100
Sugen	Pharmacia & Upjohn	6/99	$728
Sibia Neurosciences	Merck & Co.	9/99	$57 for 69% stake
CoCensys	Purdue Pharma	9/99	$7
Diatide Inc.	Schering AG	9/99**	$128
CombiChem	DuPont Pharma	10/99**	$95
Centocor Inc.	Johnson & Johnson	10/99	$4,900
Rosetta	Merck	5/01	$620

*Private company at time of transaction.
SOURCE: Information from BioVenture Consultants, BioWorld.

Forces Driving Consolidation

While the recent inflows of capital into the industry are expediting the deal flow, the primary force driving recent mergers and acquisitions is biotech companies' need to achieve critical mass. At an operating level, critical mass translates into a biotech company having sufficient cash reserves and a product pipeline deep enough for the company to weather either a prolonged equity drought or a product failure in the clinic. At a valuation level, critical mass means a company has enough current or potential revenue streams to justify its market cap. The drive to achieve critical mass seems to be affecting the strategic approaches of most biotech companies, but what form this pursuit takes depends on the type of biotech.

Take genomics and tools companies: Recognizing the need to move downstream into drug development, these companies are aggressive participants in mergers and acquisitions, and their sectors are consolidating as a result. In their deal-making campaigns, genomics and tools companies are choosing between two strategies. The first is to merge with companies that have drug development capabilities—the approach taken in recent deals between Aurora and Vertex, Rosetta and Merck, and Celera and Axys. The second strategy is to merge as a way to provide a broader offering of services—the approach that drove the recent deal between Sequenom and Gemini. It's not hard to see the inherent sense of many of these deals, but from time to time, I feel they carry the logic too far. Vertex's acquisition of Aurora, for example, solves the critical mass problem for the tools company Aurora, but I have a hard time seeing the benefit to the acquirer. It's a make-versus-buy problem—adopting the perspective of a typical drug company, it looks cheaper to rent the services of tools companies rather than to buy them, raising doubts about this kind of acquisition.

The muddled logic of a handful of deals aside, across the biotech industry I expect that the majority of the companies to be acquired in the near future will be small- and medium-size companies—in other words, biotech companies with market caps below $500 million. A few factors will make some companies more likely acquisition targets than others.

First, if a company's stock is undervalued, it will allow the potential acquirer to pay a premium and still receive a good value. Second, companies that are low on cash will usually consider a merger or acquisition, as it allows them to maintain some level of control over their futures—smart management will merge with another company before raising capital on unfavorable terms or letting the company run out of cash. A third factor that influences merger and acquisition activity is the synergy of the merging companies' programs and technologies. The Insmed-Celtrix merger in 2000 makes an excellent example, as the two companies' diabetes programs were extremely synergistic.

Almost all of the large biotech companies are actively looking for acquisitions. Chiron, for one, needs to fill up its near-term pipeline and has lots of cash available. Amgen has become more aggressive in licensing products and forming partnerships to market products for other biotech companies, and it has publicly stated an interest in making acquisitions. The genomics company Celera has become active in acquiring companies to help it make the transition to become a diversified biotech company. Millennium's acquisition of Leukosite in 1999 provided the company with its first marketed product. With its recently announced agreement to acquire Cor Therapeutics, Millennium will soon add its second product as well as expertise in cardiovascular disease. And Elan's strong history of making quick and creative decisions could lead to continued acquisitions to complement its many corporate partnerships.

Effects of Mergers and Acquisitions

Most of the time, when I have owned the stock of a company that agreed to be acquired, I felt the price being paid was too low. In some of these cases, I can look back and make a good case for this sentiment, but in many others, hindsight has given me the ability to see that investors such as myself were very fortunate that the companies were sold. Even in cases where the acquired company appeared to have been sold too cheaply, I have often done well as an investor. Besides the unexpected receipt of cash, another fortuitous outcome resulting from these transactions is that they have led me to examine anew which stocks look attractive. In the last five years, these transaction-triggered reviews have resulted in some good purchases using the proceeds from company sales.

TABLE 10.2 Biotech Acquiring Biotech

Company bought	Acquirer	Date	Price (millions)
Cytotech*	Quidel*	1989	N/A
Ingene	Xoma Corp.	1989	$40
Integrated Genetics	Genzyme Corp.	1989	$29
BioGrowth*	Celtrix	1991	$14
GlycoGen*	Cytel (now Epimmune)	1991	$6
Applied bioTechnology*	Oncogene Science (now OSI)	1991	$10
Genex	Enzon	1991	$13
Somatix*	Hana Biologics	1991	$10
Invitron	Centocor	1991	$6
Cetus	Chiron Corp.	1991	$650
Monoclonal Antibodies Inc.	Quidel*	1991	$64
Biosurface Technology*	Genzyme Corp.	12/94	$56
Synergen	Amgen Corp.	12/94	$262
Genica Pharma.*	Athena Neurosciences (now part of Elan)	2/95	$25.9
Vestar Inc.	NeXagen Inc.	2/95	$76.9
Glycomed	Ligand Pharma.	5/95	$57
Telios Pharma.	Integra LifeSciences Corp.	8/95	$35
Triplex Pharma. and Oncologix Inc.	Argus Pharma.	9/95	N/A
Viagen Inc.	Chiron Corp.	9/95	$95
Cellcor Inc.	Cytogen Corp.	10/95	$19.5
Univax Biologics Inc.	North American Biologicals Inc.	11/95	$150
Khepri Pharma*	Arris Pharma. (now Axys)	12/95	$21
Osteo Sciences Corp.*	Metra Biosystems Inc.	2/96	$10
Lexin Pharma.	Sparta Pharma.	3/96	$9.4
MYCOSearch Inc.*	Oncogene Sciences Inc.	4/96	$5
Genetrix Inc.*	Genzyme Corp.	5/96	$36.5
Rgene Therapeutics Inc.*	Targeted Genetics Inc.	6/96	$14.8
Genome Systems Inc.*	Incyte Pharmaceuticals Inc.	7/96	$7.7
ChromaXome Corp.*	Houghten Pharma.	8/96	$5.4
Combion Inc.*	Incyte Pharma.	8/96	$3

(continues)

TABLE 10.2 *(continued)*

Company bought	Acquirer	Date	Price (millions)
Aston Molecules Ltd.*	Oncogene Sciences	9/96	$2.6
NemaPharm Inc.*	Sequana Therapeutics Inc.	10/96	N/A
Innovir Labs Inc.	VIMRx Pharmaceuticals Inc.	12/96	$9 for 66%
Darwin Molecular Corp.*	Chiroscience Group plc	12/96	$120
Chemgenics*	Millennium Pharma.	2/97	$103.2
Houston Biotechnology Inc.	Medarex Inc.	2/97	$9.1
Somatix Therapy Corp.*	Cell Genesys Inc.	5/97	$85.8
Alanex Corp.*	Agouron Pharma.	5/97	$74.5
MycoTox Inc.*	Alpha-Beta Technology Inc.	6/97	$3
PharmaGenics Inc.*	Genzyme Corp.	6/97	$28
Trophix Pharmaceuticals Inc.*	Allelix Biopharmaceuticals	7/97	$23
Mercator Genetics Inc.*	Progenitor Inc.	8/97	$30
Avid Corp.*	Triangle Pharma.	8/97	$9.6
CellGenEx Inc.*	CDR Therapeutics* (became Xcyte Therapies)	9/97	ND
StemCells Inc.*	Cytotherapeutics Inc.	9/97	$7.9
GenPharm International Inc.*	Medarex Inc.	10/97	$65
Amplicon Corp.*	Tularik Inc.*	11/97	$19
Synteni Inc.*	Incyte Pharma.	1/98	$95.7
Sequana Therapeutics Inc.	Arris Pharma. (now Axys)	1/98	$118.5
VacTex Inc.*	Aquila Biopharma.	4/98	$8.2
Aptein Inc.*	Cambridge Antibody Technology Group plc	5/98	$11
Northwest Neurologic Inc.*	Neurocrine	6/98	$4.2
Virus Research Institute Inc.	T Cell Sciences Inc. (now Avant)	8/98	$150
Seragen Inc.	Ligand Pharma.	8/98	$67
Matrigen Inc.*	Prizm Pharma. (now Selective Genetics)	9/98	N/A
Hexagen plc	Incyte Pharma.	9/98	$27.7

(continues)

TABLE 10.2 *(continued)*

Company bought	Acquirer	Date	Price (millions)
ImmunoTherapy Corp.*	AVI BioPharma	9/98	$5.8
Oncormed Inc.	Gene Logic Inc.	9/98	$39
CytoMed Inc.*	UCB Pharma and Leukosite	10/98 and 1/99	$18
GeneMedicine Inc.	Megabios Corp. (now Valentis)	3/99	$38
NaviCyte Inc.*	Trega Biosciences	11/98	$6.6
ImmuLogic	Cantab Pharmaceuticals plc	2/99	$20
CellPro Inc.	Nexell Therapeutics Inc.	2/99	$3
Anergen Inc.	Corixa Corp.	2/99	$8.5
ChromaXome division of Trega	TerraGen	3/99	$6.5
polyMASC	Megabios Corp. (now Valentis)	8/99	$19.8
Roslin Bio-Med*	Geron Corp.	5/99	$26
OraVax Inc.	Peptide Therapeutics plc	5/99	$20
Prostagen Inc.*	Cytogen Corp.	6/99	$2.5
Ribi Immunochem	Corixa Corp.	6/99	$56.3
Chiroscience Group plc	Celltech plc	6/99	$528
Metra Biosystems	Quidel Corp.	6/99	$22.9
ProScript Inc.	LeukoSite Inc.	6/99	$2.73
Peptimmune Inc.*	Genzyme General	7/99	N/A
V. I. Technologies	Pentose Pharmaceuticals*	7/99	$45
RiboGene Inc.	Cypros Corp.	8/99	$13.7
Quidel Corp.	Metra Biosystems	8/99	$23
Allelix Biopharm.	NPS Pharma.	9/99*	$80
Genetic MicroSystems*	Affymetrix	9/99	$88
U.S. Bioscience	MedImmune	10/99*	$440
Enzymed	Albany Molecular	10/99	$20.6
Leukosite	Millennium	11/99	$635
Cadus	OSI Pharma.	11/99	$2.2
Celtrix	Insmed	12/99	$140
Pathogenesis	Chiron	9/00	$1.2 B

(continues)

TABLE 10.2 *(continued)*

Company bought	Acquirer	Date	Price (millions)
Megan Health	Avant Immunotherapeutics	11/00	$100
Coulter	Corixa	12/00	$200
Biomatrix	Genzyme General	12/00	
Aurora Biosciences	Vertex	4/01	$590
Gemini Genomics	Sequenom	5/01	$200
COR Therapeutics	Millenium	11/01	$1.4 B
Axys	Celera	11/01	$150
Aviron	MedImmune	12/01	$1.4 B
Immunex	Amgen	In process	$18 B

*Private company at time of transaction.
SOURCE: Information from BioVenture Consultants, BioWorld.

For example, in February 1998, Somatogen, a blood-substitute company located in Boulder, Colorado, agreed to be acquired by Baxter Labs for $9 a share. I found this disappointing, because the *Medical Technology Stock Letter* (MTSL) had recommended Somatogen in December 1992 at $18 a share, and I remained optimistic that the company would justify our recommendation. The acquisition ended all that, locking in losses of $9 a share. However, this setback turned out to have a profitable ending: With the proceeds of the Somatogen sale, MTSL purchased two stocks, ImClone Systems and ICOS Corporation. At that time, ImClone was selling at $3.50 a share (adjusting for splits), and ICOS traded at $7 (also adjusting for splits). Both stocks have been superb investments: ImClone currently trades at $70, ICOS at $60. Meanwhile, Baxter has had less luck with its acquisition, suffering through disappointing results in the clinical trials of Somatogen's lead product.

Agouron, a somewhat different story, also serves to illustrate the point. When it agreed to be acquired by Warner Lambert (now part of Pfizer) in early 1999, Agouron had just emerged as the leader in protease inhibitors to treat HIV. In addition, the company had a deep pipeline, with its lead anticancer drug having begun pivotal trials. While I thought Agouron had continuing promise as an independent company, Warner Lambert's offer was a good one. In this case, the readers of MTSL profited from the sale of a strong company. We'd recommended the stock at $2 a share in 1990 and sold during the acquisition at $60, locking in a nice profit just in time to take advantage of a mild dip in biotech stock prices, providing a number of bargain purchasing opportunities.

Summary

In 1994–1995, with the industry caught in the middle of an eight-year down cycle, industry experts predicted the demise of biotechnology as an independent sector. The popular wisdom was that large pharmaceutical companies would absorb the surviving biotech companies, essentially turning them into just another set of product lines and in-house laboratories for large pharmaceutical companies to manage. The 1999–2000 surge of capital into the industry erased these gloomy expectations. Today, large biotech companies are as well financed as they have ever been, and they are doing more deals than ever before—expanding their scale and scope by acquiring smaller biotech companies, moving into new lines of business, and forging partnerships both inside and outside the industry. As a result of the inflows of cash, biotech companies are entering into negotiations from a position of strength, negotiating better and larger deals with greater frequency than ever before. And the surge in mergers and acquisitions, rather than shrinking the industry, is galvanizing its expansion, as executives, having benefited from previous deals, work to launch new companies. The individual investor can expect the quickening pace of deal-making to continue for the next few years, as more products move through the industry's pipeline and more companies seek to reposition themselves as the competitive structure within the industry continues to change.

CHAPTER 11

Thoughts on the Future of Biotech

Thus far, in hope of illuminating the science and business of biotechnology, I've relied almost exclusively on the past and present for examples and lessons. Now it's time to do what no industry analyst can seem to resist doing: glimpse into the future. It's a poorly kept secret that in almost any field you care to mention, when it comes to imagining the future, the experts are terrific at predicting the past. It's an understandable outcome for most prognosticators—predicting is an inherently difficult business, and the natural tendency is to construct the future based on the wishful notion that current trends will continue.

When thinking about biotech's future, it's tempting to follow this pattern, but the only surefire prediction anyone can make in this industry is that the science will continue to advance. Unfortunately, this safe bet is too general to help with the problem of figuring out which companies will benefit as a result. Today's hot technologies may provide clues, but then hot technologies always look like they're going to inherit the future during their moment in the sun. Some trends continue, some trends die; in the long run, their fates are decided by unpredictable developments in science and the ensuing reactions of the markets.

Even without a crystal ball, however, there's some value in making guesses at what to expect in biotech. If you apply the fundamentals of value investing against them and change your mind as the research warrants, models of the future can help your investing approach. With this discipline in mind, I'll take a look at the future.

In terms of investing, biotech's future is taking off from a good starting point at the close of 2001. As a group, biotech stocks generally outperformed the NASDAQ and almost matched the DJIA in 2001. The advances within the sector have come without any real evidence of speculation on behalf of investors. The evidence for this is that despite the gains of larger cap biotech companies, the stocks of companies with market caps below $500 million have lagged behind. The smaller caps were under pressure all year, and they continue to offer a lot of bargain opportunities for investors.

The phenomenon of larger caps moving first, with smaller caps lagging months (or sometimes even a year or two) behind isn't new in biotech. The delayed impact of market movements on smaller caps is the result of a market perception that smaller companies carry greater fundamental risk (that is, they might run out of money or can't afford any margin of operating error). As a result of the dogged persistence of this perception in a year like 2001, when investors never lost their acute awareness of risk, the small cap stocks have yet to catch fire in the market. As I've noted earlier in the book, this kind of emotional response to the market can be frustrating—especially since the declines in prices among the smaller cap stocks have greatly reduced the real (if not the perceived) risk of these stocks. The stock prices of many of these companies are hovering somewhere just below two times their cash reserves—a tempting purchase point for a long-term value investor.

In terms of its continued development, the biotech industry has seldom, if ever, been better positioned for the future. There are a record number of drugs in Phase III clinical trials, and many exciting products are likely to gain approval in 2002. Over the next year, even more new products are likely to produce results during large Phase II trials, which will provide strong indications of their chances for eventual approval. Although not all of these products will succeed, most will generate some measure of positive results, providing more visibility even as other products are approved. In other words, the industry is going to continue to demand a lot of favorable attention and interest from Wall Street and individual investors as a result of this wave of products moving apace through trials.

So in the immediate future, the prospects for biotech continue to improve. The industry has more products in late stage clinical trials, more products in early development stages, and more robust financial resources than at any other time in its history. To get an idea of how these elements may play out further into the future, it's instructive to split the science and market perspectives and take a closer look at each.

Science

Looking at the progress of biotech in the broadest scientific terms, I think it's a safe bet to expect the industry to follow the same patterns of progress it's set for itself in the past. I think we'll continue to see the same steady, incremental advances in the science of biotech that we've witnessed all through its history. There are simply too many scientists, too many companies, and too many deep pockets in this industry to expect otherwise. In addition, because of the unprecedented resources and the sense of excitement that biotechnology can summon, the conditions have never been better for that most unpredictable and rarest of scientific events—the genuine, revolutionary breakthrough.

It's the nature of breakthroughs to ripple through the industry. As new developments and small advances build on fundamental discoveries, breakthroughs can open doors to additional opportunities long after they've been announced. For example, the impact of biotech's first fundamental breakthrough—recombinant DNA technology—has grown every year since its discovery, and will continue to do so for years to come. Recombinant DNA not only led directly to the ability to make human proteins as drugs, it also rapidly increased our knowledge about proteins and how they could be produced. Beyond enabling production of proteins as drugs, recombinant DNA allowed scientists to produce proteins to be used to screen for drugs to cure other diseases by interfering with the action of a specific protein.

Biotech is primed for more discoveries of this magnitude, and while it's anybody's guess what they may be, at least we know where they've already had the most impact. The effects of biotech's first three decades of innovation have been felt the most in medicine, with agriculture and material sciences distantly behind. For now, the bulk of the investment opportunities are in the medical sector, but it looks as though biotech, when it fulfills its promise, will broaden its scope and have an impact in more sectors of our economy than it does currently.

At present, biotech has great momentum in the medical sector. Roughly 200 products are in late-stage clinical trials, and a number of them have the potential to generate revenues in excess of $1 billion each. The greatest expectations among these potential products are for the treatment of cancer; as scientists learn to use new treatments in tandem, the promise of combination therapies only grows. In the next five to ten years, the tone of conversations about cancer may change dramatically. More rapidly effective, better-targeted treatments may appear with fewer side effects. While cures may be further off in the future (primarily because of the need to test new therapies over time), the next five to ten years could bring enough successful treatments for enough forms of cancer that many more people will live with cancer than die from it.

Also during the next five to ten years, I might expect pleasant surprises coming from some of the sectors of biotech that many investors and industry insiders have given up on. I think both gene therapy and antisense have a chance to recapture the imaginations of the scientific community as well as Wall Street, even though (to date) they've both been disappointingly slow in bringing products to market. Gene therapy and antisense may rebound as monoclonal antibodies once did, and produce a number of the blockbuster products that will be approved in the next five years. My optimism is based on the quality of the science, not current reactions of the market. Gene therapy and antisense fell victim to extravagant claims as they were introduced, and when they inevitably fell short, investors abandoned them. It always takes longer to commercialize new discoveries than anyone expects; enough time has passed and sufficient progress has been made for these sectors to merit a second look.

Looking beyond the next decade, the long-term focus of biotech may very well be on developing treatments to fight the effects of aging. Our growing understanding of how the human body regenerates itself may gradually allow us to replace and repair defective systems. One key to this possible future will be whether scientists can continue to use stem cells in their research. Another key will be how far scientists can advance their understanding of the role of the growth factors that signal tissue to repair itself, which they have already been studying for fifteen years.

Markets

In one sense, to look at how biotech will fare as an industry going forward is to look at how markets will react to inherently unpredictable future events in science. Given this condition, it's a fool's errand to drill down into the sector to pick winning stocks by relying on predictions of market trends. To find success in the markets, there's no getting around the fundamentals of value investing, which means committing to research fundamentals and monitoring the industry news as it breaks.

That said, as I think about the future of biotech markets, I believe the individual investor can reasonably expect three current trends to continue. First, it's likely that booms and painful corrections will continue to punctuate the biotech markets. As it's always done before in this sector, uncertainty over the course the science will take will influence the rises and falls. No one can predict with any certainty which companies and technologies will be involved, but the basic stories will be the same: On further inspection, revelatory technologies may not be all they're cracked up to be. Or breakthrough technologies may change the balance of power within the industry. Or innovations in science may eventually transform themselves into profitable products, but the business models haven't adapted to them yet. The savvy investor would do well to recognize the patterns of these story lines and look for them in news surrounding specific companies. In the end, no matter how many effective products with steady cash flows the industry produces across the next ten to twenty years, at its core the biotech sector is about the financing of the future and the unknown. As such, it seems unlikely that the volatility will disappear even as the industry moves into a new stage of development.

Second, the time-tested ways in which biotech stocks move through speculative cycles are likely to endure. In past rising markets, the larger capitalization stocks have tended to lead the rallies, with smaller caps lagging behind for some time before mimicking the performance of the larger caps. The market mechanism for this is relatively simple: It begins with conservative investors gravitating toward stocks of larger biotech companies that have drugs approved or on the verge of being approved. The resulting big moves in these stocks embolden investors to start looking at companies with smaller market capitalizations, particularly companies with products entering Phase III clinical trials. If some of these companies manage to bring their products through the trials and then on to market, their stocks can rise sharply. News of dramatic returns across the industry then attracts new investors, who often find it easy to get excited by companies with good stories and bid up prices of smaller, more speculative stocks (often ones with recent media coverage). Generally speaking, the longer the excitement lasts, the more substantial the subsequent declines in the market will be.

In the past, the markets have repeated this cycle over and over. When they're in the cycle's midst, it's useful to think of them as transitioning from fear to greed and then back to fear again. Investors who recognize these patterns can take advantage of them. Value investors and market timers alike can look for the broader market signals of price movements in large cap biotech companies and anticipate the inevitable fickleness at the end of the cycle as it plays out in speculation in the riskiest stocks.

Third, the biotechnology sector's current affinity for mergers and acquisitions seems likely to continue for at least the next couple of years. Most of these deals will feature larger biotech companies acquiring smaller biotech companies, mergers made more attractive by the recent popularity of the larger biotech companies, and the current bargain status of the stocks of many of the smaller companies. We also continue to see mergers of smaller biotech companies with each other. The mergers and acquisitions will help the newly hybridized companies achieve critical mass.

Despite the heightened level of deal-making activity, I expect the number of companies within the sector to continue to grow, largely (and somewhat counterintuitively) as a result of the deals themselves. Mergers and acquisitions can throw a lot of cash to investors, who often move on to new biotech investments. And deals can also inspire newly minted ex-employees to want to repeat the start-up/buyout cycle. To say that acquisitions clear the way for new biotech companies is the wrong metaphor; it's not a problem of deadwood companies being removed. Instead, deals seem to inspire those who've gone through them to reinvest and reenter the industry through new companies.

Event Risk

In attempting to present an investor's perspective, I've taken a somewhat narrow view of biotechnology as a whole. Obviously, as an area of human endeavor, biotechnology extends far beyond the boundaries of the subject of investing. Considering this and relating it back to investing, there's one element that's been overlooked thus far: event risk.

Just as the advances in biotech come from the cutting edge of the science, so do the controversies. Scientific breakthroughs are often popularly perceived through projections from science fiction, bringing more fear than understanding. For biotech investors, these perceptions create an event risk—an unforeseeable, unquantifiable risk that products and technologies might fail, not on their merits, but as a result of the public rejecting them for non-market-driven reasons.

Event risk can't be found in a company prospectus, balance sheet, or income statement. Looking at the dialogue in a typical biotech controversy, event risk seems to belong in the realm of bioethicists, academicians, politicians, journalists, sociologists, and the general public, but its impact affects the individual investor as much as it does anyone else in the equation.

Investors, like scientists, can become overly enamored of scientific discoveries, forgetting event risk. Beyond the scientific excitement, the new patentable idea, and the large market that needs treatment for a disease, there are detractors—people who believe that man shouldn't tinker with nature. When such opposing views collide, research on breakthroughs that seemed to carry promising drug development potential can be delayed or even abandoned in the face of moral and ethical debates. In controversial areas of inquiry such as abortion drugs, cloning, and stem cell research, the issues can quickly go from science and business to public relations and damage control.

For companies caught up in controversy, the effects of event risk can be striking. Consider the political crossfire that has ensnared mifepristone, popularly known as RU486. Since the drug to terminate early pregnancy first became available in France in 1988, both the manufacturer, Roussel Uclaf, and its parent, Hoechst A.G., have found themselves embroiled in an ongoing abortion debate. The companies first endured protests and boycott threats in France, then met with a 1989 FDA ban on importing RU486 for personal use in the United States, issued under pressure from antichoice members of Congress and the Bush administration. Scientists lobbied Congress, encouraging exploration of the drug's broader medical benefits in the treatment of breast cancer and other diseases where female hormones are implicated (RU486 blocks the body's use of the hormone progesterone). After President Clinton requested that the FDA reevaluate the drug, Roussel Uclaf donated the U.S. patent rights to the nonprofit Population Council. RU486 finally gained FDA approval as an abortion drug in 2000, but few patients choose it. A hostile political climate cost Roussel Uclaf and Hoechst much of the market for their product.

Currently, the biotech industry finds itself in the midst of a scientific and social debate with broad implications, carrying an element of event risk into the strategies of a number of biotech companies. At issue are stem cells, which are valued for their ability to develop into the many different specialized cell types of the body. A stem cell can become a lung cell, a skin cell, a liver cell, as directed, which means that stem cells have enormous potential for the treatment of disease. The hope is that stem cells can generate replacement cells and tissues that can be used to treat Alzheimer's disease, Parkinson's disease, spinal cord injury, stroke, burns, heart disease, diabetes, osteoarthritis, rheumatoid arthritis, and more. They also hold the possibility of creating whole organs for transplant.

In addition to their potential in creating therapies, stem cells may dramatically improve the drug development process, allowing companies to test drugs at earlier stages in more types of cells. Following such preliminary testing, qualified drugs that advanced to clinical trials would have much better chances of success.

A good portion of the debate surrounding the use of stem cells comes from their origin—typically, they're harvested from the extra embryos from fertility clinics with the permission of the couples, but sometimes they come from aborted fetuses, again with permission. The stem cells come from a part of the embryo that could not form an organism on its own, as it lacks the structures to generate a placenta and other necessary tissues.

Stem cells can also come from adult tissues—in fact, bone marrow cells are more specialized stem cells. While using an adult's own stem cells in disease treatment may prove useful in overcoming the rejection issues presented by foreign embryonic stem cells, adult cells have limitations: They don't grow or replicate as quickly as young ones (which could take too long in an acute situation), and they're less adaptable. Further, if the treatment is trying to overcome a genetic defect that's present in all of the original cells, the stem cells must be genetically engineered to fix that defect.

In late summer 2001, President Bush decided to continue federal funding for research on human stem cells, but only on cell cultures already established. Although this policy recognizes the huge area of scientific discovery ahead, it severely cripples research efforts—only ten universities and companies have such cell cultures, totaling sixty lines of stem cells. Bush defended his policy with the assertion that we shouldn't create life for the purpose of destroying it, showing his sympathy to the Catholic vote, the religious right, and other strong lobbies. His decision not to follow all reasonable lines of research does a great disservice to those who might be helped.

That's how event risk can play out in biotech—a potentially promising research path can be closed off by a presidential decision. An individual investor can avert a good deal of event risk simply by applying some common sense when approaching new technologies—certainly, looking at the origin of stem cells, it's not hard to imagine the potential for controversy. But it's also important to note that while controversies do flare up and event risk is a real factor, the odds of either affecting a particular company are low. Accounting for the social and ethical climate to safeguard against event risk is a little like checking the current weather to reduce the risk of being struck by lightning. It reduces an already infinitesimally small risk of a direct hit even further. However, if there is potential for event risk, the price of the company's stock is likely to be even more volatile, which makes buying such stocks when they are out of favor even more important.

A Few Last Words on the Big Picture

On several occasions during the course of this book, I've warned of the perils of making investment decisions based on emotion. While I believe this is sound advice, in my own case I sometimes find it hard to follow. On one hand, I'm a biotechnology investor. On the other, I'm a biotechnology enthusiast. For twenty years, I've been excited by biotech's milestone achievements, and I continue to be fascinated by the promise of its future.

On a grand scale, it looks as though biotech will emerge as the defining industry of our lifetimes. Its flagship companies are likely to inhabit the same space in the early twenty-first century that Ford, General Electric, and Bell Telephone inhabited in the early twentieth century—they have the chance to change the world and lead the markets at the same time. At some point, nearly every person alive today will have benefited from innovations that originated in biotech. The science continues to advance and expand, and the business infrastructure has rapidly matured. More companies, more patents, and more products are the tangible signs of what we can expect in the future, major breakthroughs and steady incremental advances in our knowledge of some of the fundamental problems of our time—cancer, heart disease, and the effects of aging among them. At this moment in time the industry is flush with cash, its managers have the experience to know what to do with the bounty of resources, and the markets understand the product power of biotech. The sector is poised for superior long-term returns. All you have to do is research, invest, stick by your investing philosophy, and they can be yours.

Appendix A: Biotech Companies

COMPANY	SYMBOL	12/31/01 0:00 PRICE ($)	12/31/01 0:00 MARKET CAP ($mil.)
LARGE BIOPHARMACEUTICALS			
Amgen	AMGN	56.44	59,009.1
Biogen	BGEN	57.35	8,482.1
Chiron	CHIR	43.84	8,292.0
Genentech	DNA	54.25	28,600.3
Genzyme	GENZ	59.86	12,702.1
Immunex	IMNX	27.71	15,091.9
Serono	SRA	22.19	20,122.8
BIOINFORMATICS			
Discovery Partners	DPII	7.40	179.2
Gene Logic	GLGC	18.84	503.7
GenOMIC Solutions	GNSL	2.40	58.5
Incyte	INCY	19.44	1,290.9
Lion	LEON	16.25	304.8
Pharmacopeia	PCOP	13.89	331.7
CANCER			
Abgenix	ABGX	33.64	2,896.5
Antigenetics	AGEN	16.40	541.3
Aphton	APHT	14.60	275.8
Ariad	ARIA	5.33	171.4
Biomira	BIOM	4.20	219.8
Boston Life Sciences	BLSI	2.67	55.4
British Biotech	BBIOY	2.25	149.9
Celgene	CELG	31.92	2,409.2
Cell Genesys	CEGE	23.24	804.9
Cell Pathways	CLPA	6.96	216.5
Corixa	CRXA	15.07	619.2

(continues)

COMPANY	SYMBOL	12/31/01 0:00 PRICE ($)	12/31/01 0:00 MARKET CAP ($mil.)
CANCER *(continued)*			
Cytogen	CYTO	3.01	239.0
Dendreon	DNDN	10.07	250.7
Endorex	DOR	1.03	22.9
EntreMed	ENMD	8.45	154.4
Enzon	ENZN	56.28	2,407.1
Epimmune	EPMN	3.00	30.2
Genta	GNTA	14.23	898.7
GenVec	GNVC	4.95	89.5
Genzyme Molecular	GZMO	8.00	133.8
Geron	GERN	8.70	191.7
Human Genome Sciences	HGSI	33.72	4,310.0
IDEC	IDPH	68.93	10,512.3
ImClone Systems	IMCL	46.46	3,385.8
ImmunoGen	IMGN	16.58	658.2
Immunomedics	IMMU	20.26	1,003.7
Introgen	INGN	5.54	118.8
Isis		22.19	1,044.9
Ligand	LGND	17.90	1,069.8
Maxim	MAXM	6.90	160.5
Medarex	MEDX	17.96	1,307.2
MGI	MOGN	15.28	381.3
Millennium	MLNM	24.51	6,772.3
NeoRx	NERX	5.77	153.1
Onyx	ONXX	5.12	94.8
OXiGENE	OXGN	3.07	35.1
Peregrine	PPHM	3.43	372.2
Ribozyme	RZYM	4.57	77.4
SciClone	SCLN	3.00	97.4
Seattle Genetics	SGEN	5.70	167.1
Stressgen	SSB.TO	4.60	0.0
SuperGen	SUPG	14.32	469.1
Telik	TELK	13.50	374.7
Titan	TTP	9.81	271.3
Valentis	VLTS	3.10	112.2
Vertex	VRTX	24.59	1,843.0
Vical	VICL	12.24	245.4
Vion	(mil.)	4.41	127.2
Xenova	XNVA	11.77	163.6

(continues)

COMPANY	SYMBOL	12/31/01 0:00 PRICE ($)	12/31/01 0:00 MARKET CAP ($mil.)
CARDIOVASCULAR			
Alexion	ALXN	24.44	442.8
Alteon	ALT	4.55	124.0
AtheroGenetics	AGIX	6.05	168.2
Avant Immunotherapeutics	AVAN	3.23	195.2
AVI BioPharma	AVII	10.91	252.7
BioCryst	BCRX	3.96	69.7
Collateral	CLTX	6.26	83.4
Corvas	CVAS	6.55	179.9
CV Therapeutics	CVTX	52.02	1,305.1
ICOS	ICOS	57.44	3,390.7
The Medicines Company	MDCO	11.49	397.2
Millennium	MLNM	24.51	6,772.3
Sangamo	SGMO	9.34	228.3
Scios	SCIO	23.71	1,075.7
Texas Biotech	TXBI	6.50	283.2
Valentis	VLTS	3.10	112.2
DRUG DELIVERY			
AeroGen	AEGN	3.50	70.5
Alkermes	ALKS	26.36	1,695.7
Andrx	ADRX	70.41	4,951.6
Aradigm	ARDM	7.10	209.7
Bioject	BJCT	12.59	124.0
Cygnus	CYGN	5.25	172.5
DepoMed	DMI	6.96	80.2
Elan	ELN	45.06	14,530.7
Emisphere	EMIS	31.91	566.1
Enzon	ENZN	56.28	2,407.1
Generex	GNBT	6.55	135.4
Inhale Therapeutics	INHL	18.55	1,018.6
MacroChem	MCHM	3.05	85.1
Nastech	NSTK	15.50	124.9
Noven	NOVN	17.75	398.6
Sheffield	SHM	4.69	135.7
GENE & CELL THERAPY			
Avigen	AVGN	11.51	229.7
Cell Genesys	CEGE	23.24	804.9

(continues)

COMPANY	SYMBOL	12/31/01 0:00 PRICE ($)	12/31/01 0:00 MARKET CAP ($mil.)
GENE & CELL THERAPY *(continued)*			
Collateral	CLTX	6.26	83.4
GenVec	GNVC	4.95	89.5
Geron	GERN	8.70	191.7
Introgen	INGN	5.54	118.8
StemCells	STEM	3.49	81.9
Targeted Genetics	TGEN	2.71	119.8
Valentis	VLTS	3.10	112.2
Vical	VICL	12.24	245.4
GENOMICS			
Celera	CRA	26.69	1,805.4
CuraGen	CRGN	22.37	1,089.3
Deltagen	DGEN	9.20	295.1
Exelixis	EXEL	16.62	931.1
Gene Logic	GLGC	18.84	503.6
Genome Therapeutics	GENE	6.81	155.1
Hyseq	HYSQ	7.72	147.6
Incyte	INCY	19.44	1,290.9
Large Scale	LSBC	4.50	110.6
Lynx		4.03	55.5
Myriad	MYGN	52.64	1,238.9
INFECTIOUS DISEASE			
Antex	ANX	1.55	18.9
Avanir	AVN	4.28	249.3
Avant			
Immunotherapeutics	AVAN	3.23	195.2
BioCryst	BCRX	3.96	69.6
Corixa	CRXA	15.07	619.3
Corvas	CVAS	6.55	179.9
Cubist	CBST	35.96	1,017.1
Dendreon	DNDN	10.07	250.9
Enzo Biochem	ENZ	23.50	636.5
Enzon	ENZN	56.28	2,407.1
Genome Therapeutics	GENE	6.81	155.0
Gilead Sciences	GILD	65.72	6,305.2
Hollis-Eden	HEPH	10.14	117.8
Hybridon	HYBN.OB	1.45	65.1
Immune Response	IMNR	1.34	47.1
InterMune	ITMN	49.26	1,397.6

(continues)

COMPANY	SYMBOL	12/31/01 0:00 PRICE ($)	12/31/01 0:00 MARKET CAP ($mil.)
Isis		22.19	1,044.9
Maxim	MAXM	6.90	160.5
MedImmune	MEDI	46.35	11,473.2
Nabi		10.32	392.9
Progenics	PGNX	18.47	229.3
Ribozyme	RZYM	4.57	77.3
SciClone	SCLN	3.00	97.3
Triangle	VIRS	4.01	308.0
Trimeris	TRMS	44.97	782.4
VaxGen	VXGN	11.60	165.0
Vertex	VRTX	24.59	1,843.7
Vical	VICL	12.24	245.4
ViroPharma	VPHM	22.95	429.7
INFLAMMATION			
Abgenix	ABGX	33.64	2,896.5
Alexion	ALXN	24.44	442.8
Antigenics	AGEN	16.40	541.3
Athero Genetics	AGIX	6.05	168.2
Avant Immunotherapeutics	AVAN	3.23	195.2
BioMarin	BMRN	13.44	702.7
Boston Life Sciences	BLSI	2.67	55.3
Celltech	CLL	25.01	6,868.2
Corixa	CRXA	15.07	619.2
Genelabs	GNLB	1.85	92.0
Human Genome Sciences	HGSI	33.72	4,309.4
ICOS	ICOS	57.44	3,390.4
IDEC	IDPH	68.93	10,512.2
Immune Response	IMNR	1.34	47.0
Isis	ISIP	22.19	1,044.9
La Jolla	LJPC	8.94	315.1
Millennium	MLNM	24.51	6,772.3
Protein Design Labs	PDLI	32.80	2,884.9
Regeneron	REGN	28.16	12.3
Sepracor	SEPR	57.06	4,445.2
Tanox	TNOX	18.50	815.4
Tularik	TLRK	24.02	1,195.7
Vertex	VRTX	24.59	1,842.9
XOMA	XOMA	9.85	681.6

(continues)

COMPANY	SYMBOL	12/31/01 0:00 PRICE ($)	12/31/01 0:00 MARKET CAP ($mil.)
METABOLIC DISEASES & DIABETES			
Alteon	ALTN	4.55	124.0
Amylin	AMLN	9.14	618.5
BioTech General	BTGC	8.23	479.3
BioMarin	BMRN	13.44	702.7
Genset	GENXY	2.67	65.0
Insmed	INSM	3.82	125.7
Ligand	LGND	17.90	1,069.8
Neurocrine	NBIX	51.31	1,525.8
Neurogen	NRGN	17.48	307.8
NPS Pharmaceuticals	NPSP	38.30	1,150.5
Regeneron	REGN	28.16	1,231.3
Tularik	TLRK	24.02	1,195.7
MONOCLONAL ANTIBODIES			
Abgenix	ABGX	33.64	2,896.5
Avanir	AVN	4.28	249.2
Cambridge Antibody	CATG	26.75	946.5
Corixa	CRXA	15.07	619.2
Dyax		10.97	211.4
IDEC	IDPH	68.93	10,511.9
ImClone Systems	IMCL	46.46	3,386.2
ImmunoGen	IMGN	16.58	658.2
Immunomedics	IMMU	20.26	1,003.6
Medarex	MEDX	17.96	1,307.5
NeoRx	NERX	5.77	153.2
Protein Design Labs	PDLI	32.80	2,884.8
NEUROLOGICAL			
Avanir	AVN	4.28	249.3
Boston Life Sciences	BLSI	2.67	55.4
Celgene	CELG	31.92	2,409.6
Cephalon	CEPH	75.56	3,820.9
Cortex	COR	2.58	42.9
Curis	CRIS	5.61	181.1
Elan	ELN	45.06	14,530.7
Guilford	GLFD	12.00	356.6
Interneuron	IPIC	11.09	480.0
The Medicines Company	MDCO	11.59	400.6
NeoTherapeutics	NEOT	3.66	84.1

(continues)

COMPANY	SYMBOL	12/31/01 0:00 PRICE ($)	12/31/01 0:00 MARKET CAP ($mil.)
Neurobiologics	NTII	5.10	89.3
Neurocrine	NBIX	51.31	1,525.8
Neurogen	NRGN	17.48	307.8
NPS Pharmaceuticals	NPSP	38.30	1,150.5
Pain Therapeutics	PTIE	9.16	245.7
Praecis	PRCS	5.82	297.1
Repligen	RGEN	2.43	64.7
Scios	SCIO	23.77	1,078.4
StemCells	STEM	3.49	81.9
Synaptic	SNAP	6.02	65.9
WOUND HEALING & BIOMATERIALS			
Advanced Tissue	ATIS	4.36	318.9
Carrigan	CARN	1.02	10.0
Cohesion	CSON	4.98	46.9
Curative	CURE	13.50	97.7
Curis	CRIS	5.61	181.1
Gliatech	GLIA.OB	0.85	8.2
Human Genome Sciences	HGSI	33.72	4,309.0
Integra	IART	26.34	676.6
Lifecore	LCBM	11.14	142.8
Organogenesis	ORG	4.80	177.9
Protein Poly	PPTI.OB	0.54	11.7

Appendix B: Biotech Websites and Resources

Newsletters and Industry/Business Websites

Medical Technology Stock Letter Edited by John McCamant out of Berkeley, California, this newsletter, part of the biotech scene since the early 1980s, provides nontechnical descriptions of programs and products in development and tracks the performance of a model biotech stock portfolio. Contact the company at mtsl.bioinvest.com.

www.BIO.org This web site is produced by the Biotechnology Industry Organization, the trade association that represents the biotech sector in Washington, DC, and around the world. The site contains news, information on the industry's impact (products approved, legislation, etc.), career services, and links to member company Web sites, press releases services, FDA activities, and worldwide organizations.

www.phrma.org This is the Web site for the Pharmaceutical Research and Manufacturers of America, the trade association for the big pharma companies. This group posts some very useful annual surveys on the drugs in development for specific diseases and age groups and on biotech drugs in general.

www.bioindustry.org The UK biotech industry is represented by the BioIndustry Association, which sponsors this Web site along with conferences and seminars.

www.bioventureconsultants.com *BioVenture Consultants Stock Report* (BVCSR) is published on the last Friday of each month and tracks the stock and earnings performance, market capitalization, and product status of the top 100+ public biotechnology companies. The report includes useful charts and figures that compare performance of the different biotech stock tiers versus the S&P 500, and graphically shows stock performance to date. The focus is primarily on the therapeutic and tool companies.

www.biotechinfo.com The Institute for Biotechnology Information was founded 15 years ago by Dr. Mark Dibner. Its mission is to provide strategic business information to the biotechnology, pharmaceutical, and life science communities, including databases of products in development, partnerships, market research, competitor analysis, and more. The Web site includes a free biotechnology company "phone book" that includes contact information for more than 1,500 U.S. biotech firms.

www.Biospace.com   This site combines access to the daily news wire stores and features from major business journals with original feature stores, links to sources of financial and industry news, directories of biotech companies, and chat rooms. There is also a daily "heads-up" service, called the Gene Pool, that alerts readers to key stores.

***BioWorld Today, BioWorld Financial Watch,* and Bioworld.com**   *BioWorld Today* is a daily newspaper for the biotech industry that can be obtained by fax or on-line. *BioWorld Financial Watch*, published weekly via fax and on-line, covers the top financial and corporate partnering stories and provides and overview of the biotech stock performance. BioWorld.com provides on-line access to current and archived issues of both publications, as well as special reports on the industry and market activity info. Contact the company at info@bioworld.com or at 800.688.2421.

Windhover Information, www.windhoverinfo.com   This publishing group produces *In Vivo* magazine (industry trends, key developments, company strategies in the biomedical/device/equipment/hospital supply/diagnostic industries; *Start Up Magazine* (focus on emerging medical markets and young companies); *Health Care Strategies* (an annual review of deal-making activity and trends, the most active banks and companies, and other important aspects of business development); *Pharmaceutical Strategic Alliances* (an annual summary review of pharmaceutical deals); and Strategic Intelligence Systems (a computer-based subscription that allows you to monitor business and financial activity in the biopharmaceutical world). Several of these publications are available in print and on-line. Contact the company at 203.838.4401x232 or email: custserv@windhoverinfo.com.

www.recap.com   Recombinant Capital, based in San Francisco, California, has an interesting Web site that combines original features with access to its own databases on products in clinical development and corporate partnerships. The company also hosts an annual meeting, the Allicense Conference, that provides a great overview of the corporate partnering issues and trends of the previous year.

www.bioportfolio.com/bio   This site, organized by Bioportfolio Ltd., in Cambridge, England, includes a database of 5,500 global biobusinesses with 20,000 hyperlinks to stockbroker reports, news services, stock prices, the U.S. Patent Office, and company Web sites. The site is aimed primarily at companies needing information to support strategic analysis.

www.genengnews.com   *Genetic Engineering* news publishes a newsletter and this Web site, which includes daily biotech news from press releases.

PJB Publications   This UK-based biopharmaceutical publishing house produces a number of relevant newsletters and magazines, including the monthly *BioVenture View* (not related to BioVenture Consultants), *Biopeople Magazine*, and *Biocommerce Data Ltd*. Contact the company at www.pjbpubs.co.uk or call 212.262.8230.

www.techvestllc.com/newsletter   Techvest LLC publishes a newsletter for individual investors interested in biotech and biomedical investments. A subscription form is on the Web site.

www.sec.gov/agi-bin/srch-edgar   This site provides access to SEC documents filed by companies.

Other Sites

www.fda.gov   This site gives you access to the Food and Drug Administration's full court press of information on regulations, upcoming advisory panel meetings, and events.

www.nih.gov   The National Institutes of Health are the primary federally funded health care research institutes. This site will take you to all of the individual institutes, including the National Cancer Institute, and provides access to information on diseases, research, and ongoing clinical trials.

www.biomednet.com   The Internet community for biological and medical researchers, including a daily news-and-views service, links to a huge database of medical and scientific Web sites, career services, access to the 9 million records in a free MEDLINE database of scientific articles, reports from scientific conferences, and all sorts of cool stuff!

www.aaas.org   This site is the Web site of the American Association for the Advancement of Science. The AAAS publishes a highly regarded scientific journal—although the articles are way beyond non-science-nerds, the overview of current events on the site and the interesting topics in www.scienceon-line.org, the AAAS's companion site, can provide a window into the most recent scientific advances and politics.

www.bis.med.jhmi.edu/Dan/DOE/intro.html   "A Primer on Molecular Genetics," published by the Department of Energy (which funds the Human Genome Project). The site provides definitions of important terms.

www.citeline.com   This San Francisco-based service allows you to search for information on different diseases, along with articles on treatments.

www.Drkoop.com   This site gives you access to medical encyclopedias, disease directories, and basic health information.

www.med.upenn.edu/-bioethic   This site is sponsored by the Center for Bioethics at the University of Pennsylvania, and it links to pages covering many different areas of the impact of technology on biology and the ethical implications.

www.gene.com/ae   The Academic Excellence site, maintained by Genentech, contains information, news, and activities, for teachers and students.

www.cellsalive.com   This site has color images of cells and bacteria.

Index